COACHING CHEERLEADING SUCCESSFULLY

Linda Rae Chappell

Human Kinetics

Library of Congress Cataloging-in-Publication Data

Chappell, Linda Rae, 1947-
Coaching cheerleading successfully / Linda Rae Chappell.
p. cm.
Includes index.
ISBN 0-87322-942-8
1. Cheerleading. I. Title.
LB3635.C53 1997
791.6'4--dc20 96-3038
CIP

ISBN: 0-87322-942-8

Figure 5.5 was adapted, with permission, from *Preparticipation Physical Evaluation*, 1992, by the American Academy of Family Physicians, the American Academy of Pediatrics, the American Medical Society for Sports Medicine, the American Orthopaedic Society for Sports Medicine, and the American Osteopathic Academy of Sports Medicine.

Acquisitions Editor: Jim Kestner; **Developmental Editor:** Jessie Daw; **Assistant Editor:** Lynn M. Hooper; **Editorial Assistant:** Coree Schutter; **Copyeditor:** Judith Kirkwood; **Proofreader:** Pam Johnson; **Indexer:** Theresa J. Schaefer; **Graphic Artist:** Denise Lowry; **Graphic Designers:** Keith Blomberg and Judy Henderson; **Photo Editor:** Boyd LaFoon; **Cover Designer:** Jack Davis; **Cover Photo:** Dave Black; **Mount Photographer (chapter 8):** Debbie Sauer; **Illustrator:** Bridgette McElwee Waldau; **Printer:** Versa Press

Copies of this book are available at special discounts for bulk purchase for sales promotions, premiums, fund-raising, or educational use. Special editions or book excerpts can also be created to specifications. For details, contact the Special Sales Manager at Human Kinetics.

Printed in the United States of America 10 9 8 7 6 5

Human Kinetics
Web site: www.humankinetics.com

United States: Human Kinetics, P.O. Box 5076, Champaign, IL 61825-5076
800-747-4457
e-mail: humank@hkusa.com

Canada: Human Kinetics, 475 Devonshire Road, Unit 100, Windsor, ON N8Y 2L5
800-465-7301 (in Canada only)
e-mail: hkcan@mnsi.net

Europe: Human Kinetics, P.O. Box IW14, Leeds LS16 6TR, United Kingdom
+44 (0)113 278 1708
e-mail: humank@hkeurope.com

Australia: Human Kinetics, 57A Price Avenue, Lower Mitcham, South Australia 5062
08 8277 1555
e-mail: liahka@senet.com.au

New Zealand: Human Kinetics, P.O. Box 105-231, Auckland Central
09-309-1890
e-mail: hkp@ihug.co.nz

This book is dedicated to the rowdy East Texas cheerleader I married many years ago, William "Sage" Sengbush, and to our two beautiful children, Megan Chappell Sengbush and Ray Chappell Sengbush. Thanks for cheering me on!

Contents

Foreword

Coaching Cheerleading Successfully is the most comprehensive book on cheerleading that I have ever read. Every aspect of cheerleading is covered; coaches in small school districts, rural communities, or large urban communities all will find something helpful to their area of the country. Linda Rae Chappell supplies the tools for a cheerleading coach to create a great squad for whatever type of cheerleading is wanted, from competition squads to regular cheering, from cheerleaders who are ambassadors of school spirit and sportsmanship to those who are student leaders. This book builds on the age-old basics of cheerleading, bringing them up to the present and taking them into the future. It is all here in *Coaching Cheerleading Successfully.*

I particularly like Linda's materials on general philosophy, motivational techniques, and teaching leadership skills. And I like her emphasis on service to the student body and community and on the techniques for the proper performance of the many athletic skills required in cheerleading routines. Safety and conditioning are also well covered.

Reading *Coaching Cheerleading Successfully* is a must for novice cheerleading coaches, and even veteran coaches will find it a source of constant reference. I encourage you to read and learn from this valuable book. I am sure you will refer to it often for fresh ideas, and you will be a much better coach for having read it.

Lawrence "Herkie" Herkimer

Founder, National Cheerleaders Association (America's first cheerleading company)

Acknowledgments

I am so very thankful for the myriad of positive experiences that have illuminated my cheerleading life! These experiences are intertwined in the lives of my family and friends, who have made it possible for me to serve others. In the spirit of gratitude, I would like to thank:

My mom, Virginia Lee Chappell, for believing in me and inspiring me to believe in myself.

My dad, Bill Chappell, for validating my intelligence and instilling in me the importance of integrity.

My sisters Laura Lee Westhues and Lisa May Redel for their encouragement and validation.

My namesake niece, Linda Lee Cottle, for making work and fun the same thing.

My brother Randy Chappell for his friendship, humor, and reminders of "the real world."

Beed Harris, Heather Reynolds, and Karole Hart, for sharing their friendship, dedication, and skill on many projects.

Nancy Knipfel and Suzy Thompson for exemplifying "building people through cheerleading."

Susan True, for pioneering the validation of cheerleaders as athletes, and for advancing the level of safety education.

Lawrence "Herkie" Herkimer, for remaining committed to his original vision, and for his leadership, integrity, and honest friendship.

Kay Crawford, whose unselfish service to thousands of young people has been a vital source of inspiration to me.

Jessie Daw, developmental editor at the American Sport Education Program, for her patience, guidance, and support in preparing this book for publication.

Thanks to thousands of special coaches and cheerleaders across the country who continue to serve their schools through dedication and leadership in spite of terrific challenges.

Thanks to the hundreds of former professional cheerleading camp instructors across the country who worked for me from 1971 to 1993. You not only had a dynamic impact on my life, you are shining lights in my world! I will carry you gently in my heart forever.

Introduction

I am honored to have been asked by the American Sport Education Program to write a foundation book for cheerleading coaches. My love for cheerleading began in the early 1960s at Raytown South High School in Raytown, Missouri, and continued at Central Missouri State University in Warrensburg, Missouri. My experience working with coaches and cheerleaders began in college in 1968 when I started teaching at summer cheerleading camps across the country. In 1971, I started my own cheerleading company, Dynamic Cheerleaders Association, which I managed until 1993.

In *Coaching Cheerleading Successfully*, I present a culmination of over 30 years of cheerleading and coaching experience. Every aspect of cheerleading is explained in this book. You will find personal stories, examples, tips, creative ideas, illustrations, photographs, and sample forms to help you every step of the way.

Part I explains the foundations of coaching a cheer program—philosophy, communication, motivation, and organization. Next, Part II helps you make effective coaching plans for the season and for practices. Skill development is a crucial part of your program, so I have included extensive explanations of cheerleading basics, safety issues, and stunting in Part III. Part IV covers how to coach for athletic events, how to build school spirit, and how to prepare for cheer camps and competitions. Part V focuses on how to evaluate yourself, your cheerleaders, and your program. Finally, Appendix A offers you valuable information about how you and your squad can develop your own cheerleading constitution, and Appendix B includes the names and addresses of cheerleading resources across the country.

The goals that I have for *Coaching Cheerleading Successfully* are very important to me. I hope this book

- helps novice cheerleading coaches learn how to establish and lead a squad effectively,
- offers experienced coaches ideas about how to improve their existing programs,
- helps both new *and* experienced cheerleading coaches gain confidence in and build respect for their programs,
- aids coaches in the important task of helping their cheerleaders serve their schools and communities,
- enhances creativity, skill, fun, and friendship,
- accentuates positive leadership and cheering safety, and
- helps coaches learn how to "build people through cheerleading."

It means a lot to me that I am offering ideas and suggestions—based on my own experiences—that will help you establish a unique program that you can all your own. You need to feel confident in your leadership role and feel comfortable that you are doing your best for your cheerleaders. I hope *Coaching Cheerleading Successfully* will become your friend in your quest for effective coaching.

Writing this book for cheerleading coaches across the country has given me the opportunity to serve those who serve young leaders. I am truly grateful to be able to give back a little of what I have received from the thousands of coaches and cheerleaders who have brightened my days and shown me the way.

Part I

Coaching Foundation

Chapter 1

© CLEO Photography

Developing a Philosophy

To coach cheerleaders successfully, you must have the heart for the job. Since your primary responsibility is to build the person *through* cheerleading, your heart should be filled with love and care before the first coaching technique is introduced.

I have worked with thousands of cheerleaders over 25 years of coaching, from little ones at the YMCA to those at the NFL professional level. They are special and unique and rowdy, and I love 'em. I have befriended them as I have coached them. I've hugged them and helped them through their struggles. They've climbed on me, confided in me, cried with me. And many times I have soothed their jangled nerves. I love cheerleaders because they cheer from their hearts. They keep going . . . and going . . . and going.

If I am asked how cheerleading has changed over the years that I have been in coaching, I always begin by saying that I feel that the soul of cheerleading remains untouched:

- The excitement of winning a spot on the squad
- The determination to prepare for the season
- The exhilaration of the first game's performance
- The realization of spirit and accomplishment
- The celebration of friendship and love

While the heart and soul of cheerleading have remained the same, the challenges, the changes, and the choices have not. Sexist stereotypes still exist and some people still think cheerleading is not athletic. The truth is, males and females can cheer side by side as both athletes and student leaders, advancing skill levels to even greater heights. And while traditional cheerleading continues to flourish, competitive cheer has developed into a sport of its own.

Cheerleading has evolved past the negative stereotype of clueless cute girls bouncing up and down on the sidelines. Cheering in the 21st century promises even more excitement because males and females are developing their athletic abilities along with their leadership skills to provide good role models for all of America's youth.

In this chapter, I will discuss coaching philosophies and their objectives. My aim is to help you develop your own coaching philosophy and your own objectives as you learn how to coach cheerleaders successfully.

What Is a Philosophy?

Your philosophy is your foundation: all decisions you make as a coach will result from this foundation. Many coaches really don't take the time to consider what their philosophy is. But since your philosophy is the basis for all decisions and actions, examining it is one of the most important things you can do as a coach. By having a solid grasp of your coaching philosophy, many tough decisions will be easier to make, and your cheerleaders will benefit by having a coach who is consistent in addressing important aspects of the squad.

Ultimately, your philosophy must be your own. One coach's set of values will not be another's. Certainly as you reflect on and refine your philosophy, you will realize that much of it is drawn from experiences you or significant others in your life have had. Whether consciously or not, you have probably borrowed things here and there from those who have influenced your life in some way. The things I share that are important to my philosophy may be important to yours as well. The most important point, though, is that you spend time thinking about your philosophy. Your philosophy leads to your objectives, and your objectives lead to your decisions. When you spend time developing and reflecting on your philosophy, decisions will be easier to make.

The task of developing and reflecting on a philosophy is not easy. I ask myself the following three questions in order to reevaluate my priorities and learn more about myself through introspection:

- What do I believe?
- Who do I befriend?
- How do I behave?

After I answer these questions and establish my priorities, I begin to develop my philosophy around three key coaching issues: authenticity, commitment, and perspective. I occasionally take a personal inventory in these three areas to help me stay grounded in my philosophy. Through the years, I have developed a set of Dominant Thought cards, which I refer to quite often (especially when I need some gentle reminders). The Dominant Thought cards are positive affirmations that not only pinpoint my personal approach to life but also anchor me to what is most important in my life. I hear my own voice when I read them, and I am immediately connected to my beliefs. I have eight affirmations for each of my three key areas.

The Foundation of My Personal Philosophy: Dominant Thoughts

AUTHENTICITY

My life is my message.

I communicate from my authentic self.

As I give, I receive.

I shine with my own special spirit.

I accept myself just as I am.

I communicate truth in my words and actions.

I experience life fully in the present moment.

I am free to change and to grow.

COMMITMENT

I am responsible for creating my own experience.

My rewards in life equal the quality of my service.

I face my circumstances with confidence and a good attitude.

I am willing to work hard for what I believe in.

I use my fullest abilities in pursuit of excellence.

I move in the direction of my dominant thoughts.

I set a good example by meeting situations with enthusiasm.

My personal mission is to share my love.

PERSPECTIVE

I look for the light in all people and situations.

I stay centered with positive thoughts and expectations.

I treat people with patience and respect.

I look for strengths in myself and others.

I can plant seeds of peace, joy, and happiness today.

I am not afraid to take risks.

I have the ability to make a positive impact.

I can create the best life I can envision.

Authenticity

For me, to know myself and be me is very important to coaching success and my philosophy. When I am in tune with who I am, accepting of my strengths and weaknesses, it is easier to relate with my cheerleaders because I can then see them for who they are. Also, actions speak louder than words, so how I "live my message" helps me to be authentic around my cheerleaders. For instance, talking about being thoughtful to each other doesn't send home the message as much as when I give little spirit presents or appreciation notes. Since being kind and thoughtful are important to my personal philosophy, I make sure that my actions toward my cheerleaders reflect this belief.

NEVER TOO OLD FOR SPIRIT PRESENTS

I coached the Kansas City Chiefs' Coed Professional Cheerleading Squad for four years. The squad members ranged from 19 to 28 years old. I had been used to giving spirit presents to elementary, junior high, and high school cheerleaders, so I continued the tradition with the Chiefs. I would bring them buttons, pins, carnival items, and positive quotations, each one with a special slogan relating to cheering, friendship, or spirit. Often, I would encounter silence, muffled laughs, or sarcastic smirks when giving them. I decided one day that maybe the Chief cheerleaders were too old for spirit presents, so I stopped bringing them. At the end of practice, one of the older male cheerleaders raised his hand and asked, "Don't we get spirit presents today?" It wasn't until that moment that I truly realized that people are never too old for spirit presents, and, even if they don't show it, they appreciate the meaning and the thoughtfulness. (It's been 10 years since I coached the Chief cheerleaders, and some of them have reported to me that they still have their spirit presents.)

Some other things to think about as you consider authenticity include being honest with yourself, your cheerleaders, and others with whom you work. This includes admitting and taking responsibility for mistakes, as well as facing issues you may be struggling with. When you are honest with your cheerleaders, this openness will provide fertile ground for building teamwork and cohesion. At times you will be angry in front of your cheerleaders. Even though this is a difficult situation, I recommend that you be honest with your cheerleaders about your anger, apologize if you need to, and do the best job you can to explain your feelings. This is an excellent opportunity for your cheerleaders to see how to appropriately handle anger.

Commitment

An important part of my philosophy deals with commitment. I have always felt that a successful cheerleading coach must be committed to nurturing and building the lives of young people. My commitment stems from a philosophical viewpoint of cheerleading participation having the potential of enhancing self-confidence and self-esteem. When you view all members of your squad as individuals who have the potential to improve their physical skills and develop their confidence, you can make a commitment to help each reach his or her potential. These internal rewards of coaching can be some of the most powerful.

Because cheerleading offers a myriad of experiences, a good coach realizes that "building people through cheerleading" entails emphasizing positive values, responsibility, and dedication. Your cheerleaders will judge by your actions whether you are committed to them and the program. Your punctuality, organization, respectful communication, and rapt attention let them know you are committed to them. Coaches can provide an excellent environment for nurturing personal growth by communicating positive values through their behaviors. By emphasizing personal growth as part of a philosophy, coaches will find it easy to make decisions in the best interest of their cheerleaders.

Perspective

The third important part of my philosophy is perspective. The job of coaching cheerleaders can be extremely demanding, and it is easy to lose sight of the bigger picture if you get bogged down in the details of keeping the program running smoothly. Keeping the activity in perspective helps both you and your cheerleaders remember that cheerleading is not life—even though it offers many valuable experiences that contribute to the development of the individual. As a coach, I find it helpful to remember that I cannot please everyone, I will make mistakes, and I will sometimes be frustrated. Having a philosophy that helps me keep things in perspective allows me to move beyond these problems and make helping my cheerleaders grow the first priority.

I still stay in contact with many of my former cheerleaders from the 1970s and 1980s. They remind me of the positive impact that cheerleading has made on their lives. Some of them talk about overcoming shyness and low self-esteem, about working harder for better grades, about the value of enthusiasm in the workplace, and about taking greater responsibility for health and fitness later in life. They say that their high school and college careers were more enriching because of their involvement in cheerleading and school spirit. They tell me—and it's true—the memories last forever.

CHEERLEADING AT THE CROSSROADS: WHAT DO PEOPLE WANT?

My philosophy was severely tested during a time when I had been coaching a professional, coed cheerleading squad for an NFL football team. I had made a commitment to provide wholesome, athletic entertainment and leadership at the stadium for every home game. My squad was comprised of 12 males and 12 females who exemplified the highest level of cheerleading skill and whose appearance and performance were geared for family viewing. After four years, the management decided to replace the coed squad with a scantily clad dance team. Since my coaching philosophy is deeply rooted in my personal philosophy of living the message of high standards and presenting cheerleaders as good role models, I could not be a part of or support this departure from the original vision of "wholesome, athletic entertainment and leadership." As the public found out about the change, letters of protest were sent to the corporate office, and the coed squad was reinstated (under someone else's leadership). They were replaced four years later with an all-female dance team. Wholesome, athletic entertainment lost out to the showgirl image perpetuated at many professional games. Is this what the people really want?

Establishing Your Objectives

What are objectives and why are they important? The connection between philosophy and objectives is that philosophy tells "why" and objectives tell "what." The objectives of your cheerleading program are the goals of your program, and they are important because they give action to your philosophy. It is very important to take the time to establish your coaching objectives so that you can stay consistent with your philosophy and so that you can evaluate the effectiveness of your program. As you put together a cheerleading squad for the first time, or evaluate an existing program, it is important to look at cheerleader objectives and squad objectives, as well as personal objectives for coaches.

Cheerleader Objectives

When you begin to think about cheerleader objectives, ask yourself how the individual cheerleaders benefit from your program. What actions will you take to establish a positive experience and to represent your philosophy of coaching? Almost everything that happens during the days of cheerleading can transcend the experience. By that I mean that the individual cheerleader can gain valuable experiences that will impact later years.

Here are five of the cheerleader objectives that I feel are most important:

1. To develop physical skills and to learn about personal conditioning, good health habits, and safety
2. To develop psychologically through increased self-confidence, self-esteem, and emotional maturity
3. To develop socially through cooperation, competition, and appropriate standards of behavior
4. To make a serious commitment to academics
5. To develop effective time management strategies

These cheerleader objectives are not easily tested or measured, but should be monitored as part of your program evaluation. They form a foundation for the actions you will take as coach. As you begin to develop your own cheerleader objectives, keep in mind what is most important to you regarding the skills and qualities that you think cheerleaders should learn. The objectives you select for your program will evolve from your personal philosophy, the type of squad you are coaching, and the role your cheerleaders have in your school and community.

Squad Objectives

I feel it is important to establish squad objectives to further support and communicate your philosophy. Besides providing a structure for the foundation of your program, having squad objectives will ensure that your squad will be working toward the same goals. Often, it is easier for cheerleaders to understand your objectives than your philosophy. The squad objectives that I consider most important are teamwork, supporting your school, and competition.

Teamwork

Working as a team builds group cohesion and a commitment to common goals. After you have established an objective, you will need to back it up by the structure of your program. For instance, working as a team is important to me because I feel that building group cohesion and squad unity is crucial to the growth of the individual (the "commitment" part of my personal philosophy). As the team member becomes more comfortable within the squad, the person will have more confidence to try new ideas, will not be afraid to make a mistake, and can feel a bond of friendship or a sense of belonging. All of these reactions help nurture opportunities to expand the feeling of group unity.

Some of the ways I strive to meet this squad objective are to hold special events, set goals as a group, practice communication exercises, and discuss the qualities of good leaders. I also stress the importance of the cheerleaders being good role models in the school and community by becoming involved in service projects or spirit-building events.

Supporting Your School

Cheerleaders exist because of school sports programs. Supporting the school's sports programs is a very important squad objective because skill, leadership ability, or school spirit alone will not make a good cheerleading squad. School support—*along with* squad unity, leadership ability, and school spirit—will make a successful cheerleading squad. Supporting the school's athletic programs is the primary purpose of having cheerleading squads in the first place, and that's why this squad objective is so important to me.

After establishing the squad objective to support the school's sports programs, it is important to answer the question: What sports do we cheer for? Sometimes this can be a tough issue. The goals, decisions, and objectives established will have a major impact on your cheerleading program. Here are a few of the many factors to evaluate when deciding which sports will have cheerleaders and which ones will not:

- Size and population of the school
- Number of girls and boys sports offered
- School traditions
- Finances
- Interest in cheerleading
- Community support for athletic programs
- Coaching availability
- Appropriateness of cheering at some athletic events

After these factors have been evaluated, there are many choices to consider when deciding what sports to cover. Here are some of the squad options that schools have used:

- Only varsity teams have cheerleaders at their games.
- Each team has a separate squad.
- Each squad covers specific sports for specific seasons.
- One large squad divides up and covers many sports.
- A combination of the above is used.

When you consider how many and which sports to support, keep Title IX in mind. The Office of Civil Rights (OCR) of the Department of Education—responsible for "enforcement" of Title IX—considers whether programs are equitable; they review if cheerleader support is given for the same number of girls' teams as boys' teams.

Many smaller schools have one or two squads for all of the sports. And many of the larger schools have multiple squads, each one cheering for a different sport or during a different season. You should meet with your school administrators and athletic coaches to discuss all the factors before deciding how your cheerleaders will effectively support as many sport teams as possible. The role of your cheerleaders within the school community, for example, needs to be discussed. The possibilities span from one squad "doing it all" to multiple squads, each serving one team. Cheerleaders provide an important service to the school, and I advocate some kind of support for every sport team represented in the school, through game cheering, posters, banners, pep rallies, or individual spirit boosters.

Competition

In some parts of the country, two different types of cheerleading squads are common: cheerleaders and competitive cheer squads. Cheerleaders provide crowd leadership, spirit, and support of the school's athletic programs. Competitive cheer squads compete against other cheer squads in front of a set of judges. In some schools, cheerleaders and competitive cheer squads are the same group. Cheerleading and competitive cheer squads can successfully coexist, and this is happening all over the country.

Competition has a different focus, and your objectives will reflect different choices. In competition, the objectives for cheering center on learning and perfecting skills, such as jumps, pyramids, and tumbling. Mastering cheering basics such as precision, timing, voice control, execution, and spirit projection becomes the primary focus of the program, since the squad will be judged on every key aspect of skilled performance. The competitive squad will not be leading a crowd, so the emphasis is on technique and measurable skill execution.

If you have one squad that is both a cheerleading squad and a competitive cheer squad, you may be faced with some tough decisions: Do you support the team on game night or do you attend the competition? Do you make posters and banners or do you practice for competition? The answers to these dilemmas will reflect your personal philosophy and objectives. Which direction will you take?

Coach Objectives

I feel it is important for cheerleading coaches to establish personal objectives because the role of a coach is so important in the lives of squad members. Your coaching objectives provide the structure for your entire program. They are your starting points and reference points. They direct your action. The action you take will result from two areas: your knowledge and your facilitation.

Knowledge

Cheerleading coaches need to make informed choices on how to build a program that is consistent with a personal philosophy. To be comfortable running your own program, you should collect as much information as possible (such as how to conduct tryouts, how to run practices, how to build skills, etc.) before deciding on a course of action. You can gather valuable information from books and tapes, as well as from seminars, conventions, workshops, clinics, and camps. Then evaluate the ideas in reference to personal style, practicality, and squad enhancement. Only you will know what will work for your specific circumstances.

Your past experience can be used as a tool to enhance your knowledge. You bring many important life experiences to your position as a cheerleading coach. Draw on your own personal history to help you become the coach you want to be. Since your objectives stem from your philosophy and establish your action, you will be able to take action based on your past experiences. You can gain insight into your personal management style by talking with a few friends or family members to obtain feedback. Learning from experience means that you can take action based on insight and information. Almost any life experience contains the seeds for learning how to be a better coach.

MY GREATEST TEACHER

I had already been working with cheerleaders for over 10 years when my multihandicapped son, Ray, was born. Since Ray had cerebral palsy and was deaf, we faced many challenges as he grew up. With the help of therapists, we continue to encourage him to develop his potential to become all that he can. This is the same philosophy that has helped me as a coach. One of the reasons Ray is so outgoing and happy is that he grew up with cheerleaders around him all the time. Through my experiences with my son over the years, I have developed a deeper love and greater patience; I have learned to focus on and enjoy the present moment and to accept and adjust to individual differences. Not only does Ray have a positive impact on my life each day, his message is important for all coaches.

Facilitation

I have selected facilitation as an important personal objective because my most important goal in all I do is to become a facilitator of learning. I feel responsible for developing my capabilities through study and experience: I facilitate my learning by reading, taking classes, and listening to the people in my world. As I learn, I can enjoy helping others to learn, by sharing my experiences, conducting seminars, and sending newsletters.

Being a facilitator means being both student and teacher: Communication comes full circle when the teacher learns from the student and the student learns from the teacher. To facilitate learning means to provide opportunities for growth, discovery, development, and success. I have come to cherish the immeasurable rewards of making a difference in someone's life by facilitating their learning.

PASS IT ON

One of my cheerleading students from many years ago brought me up to date on what she was doing with her life. She went into many details about becoming a teacher and the ideas and exercises she was using with her students. I commented that I was very proud of her and excited about her success. She looked up at me, and in a quiet voice said, "Linda, I'm doing the things I learned from you. Thank you for touching my life."

The most important thing to remember here is to take the time to evaluate your coaching objectives and focus in light of your personal coaching philosophy. I selected knowledge and facilitation as my objectives because they have special meaning to the expression of my individuality.

Summary

The following are the key points to consider when establishing your coaching philosophy and objectives:

- All decisions you make as a coach will result from your philosophy.
- Ultimately, your philosophy must be your own.
- Three key areas to consider when thinking about your philosophy are authenticity, commitment, and perspective.
- Take time to establish coaching objectives because they are the goals of your program and give action to your philosophy.
- To develop physically, psychologically, socially, and academically are examples of important cheerleader objectives.
- Teamwork, supporting your school, and competition are important squad objectives.
- You will need to decide which sports to cheer for after evaluating issues such as the number of sports offered, school traditions, number of cheerleading squads, and availability of coaching.
- In some parts of the country, there are two different types of cheerleading squads—cheerleaders and competition cheer squads. Sometimes these two roles are shared by the same squad. Establish objectives for each type.
- The personal objectives that I feel are important for coaches are knowledge and facilitation.

Chapter 2

Communicating Your Approach

The quality of your program is directly influenced by the quality of your communication. My goal in this chapter is to help you understand how to communicate effectively with the faculty, the sport team coaches, the parents, the student body, the local community, and your cheerleaders. In order for your program to make a positive impact in the school, the community, and in the lives of your cheerleaders, you must try to establish open communication lines. By this I mean that you routinely distribute information, ask for feedback, and involve everyone in the process of making things happen.

Communicating With Cheerleaders

"Let's do that last cheer again. Line it up!" came a voice from the middle of the group.

The coach sat on the second row of bleachers, grading papers.

"O.K. Jump circle. We're going to work on our toe touches!" came a voice from the middle of the group.

The coach sat on the second row of bleachers, grading papers.

"That last pyramid needs some more work.

O.K. bases, line it up!" came a voice from the middle of the group.

The coach stood up on the second row of bleachers, glanced at the clock, and said hurriedly, "Practice is over. Good job. See you tomorrow."

"Who's THAT?" came a whisper from the middle of the group.

Communicating with your cheerleaders means being present both mentally and physically. It means words spoken with knowledge and care. It means proximity, focus, concern, involvement. It means body language, tone of voice, eye contact. It means listening thoughtfully and speaking thoughtfully.

We naturally use words to communicate, but it's action that delivers the message. Cheerleaders learn more by what you do than by what you say. Your nonverbal messages often speak louder than your verbal ones. Remember that how you say something to your cheerleaders will be just as important as what you say. Good communication skills will often be your most important key to success with your squad.

In working with cheerleaders, I have found it helpful to remember the following basic communication guidelines: develop a personal relationship, be honest, have a positive attitude, be self confident, have an open-door policy, provide appropriate feedback, celebrate, avoid comparisons, and be respectful. I will discuss each one briefly.

Develop a Personal Relationship

It's important to establish a personal relationship with all squad members, showing an interest in their families, unique talents, and goals. The more you can get to know each cheerleader as an individual, the better your communication will be. If and when extenuating circumstances crop up, such as a family crisis, you will be able to understand more fully how to deal with the situation (or how to help your cheerleader deal with the situation). You will have a better understanding of why your cheerleaders act the way they do and you will be able to be a better listener and more compassionate if you are able to know your cheerleaders as people first, cheerleaders second. Communication can occur on a more meaningful level once rapport is established. Some coaches prefer to communicate in a strictly nonpersonal way, from the role of coach to athlete, and you will need to decide how you are comfortable.

Be Honest

Always be yourself. Even if you do not have tons of personal confidence about what you are doing, try to relax and just be honest about everything. If you are comfortable with yourself, you will make it much easier for your cheerleaders to relax and be honest with you. If you don't know something or if you have made a mistake, always admit it. Your personal honesty and integrity determine your true self, and they will consequently have a profound impact on your communication with your cheerleaders.

Have a Positive Attitude

When communicating with your cheerleaders, keep an upbeat attitude and accentuate the positive. Your positive approach will enhance communication because you will have turned on the light, opened up possibilities (maybe humor), and invited a positive response. You will have many opportunities to establish the mood in a circumstance just by your tone of voice, facial expression, or upbeat words. Your positive attitude will help solve problems and keep things in perspective. Don't allow your cheerleaders to focus on negatives or get carried away with petty complaints. Attitudes are contagious!

NEW BEGINNINGS

My friend had been coaching the number-one cheerleading squad in her division in the state for many years. And, as many coaches experience at some point, she had "lost" all of her experience, as well as her talent, after graduation. She was starting over (in cheerleading, it's called a "rebuilding year"). I knew that she faced many challenges coaching her young squad to competition status. And through the many months of preparation, she sometimes had difficulty maintaining a positive attitude.

As the date for the state competition approached, I spoke with her and asked how everything was going. She said, "Linda, I have really learned a lot from my squad this year. Even though they worry about not doing as well as previous squads from our school, they have been very positive about working hard and doing their best at the competition. They tell me regularly that 'it's time for a new beginning.' They have helped me remember the importance of squad unity, teamwork, and positive attitudes. Not only is it a new beginning for them, it's also a new beginning for me. I needed to be reminded to keep competition in its proper perspective."

Be Self-Confident

When talking to your cheerleaders, communicate with self-confidence, which is a by-product of a firm sense of self. You will serve as a role model for your cheerleaders in many different ways. You can help them develop self-confidence by exemplifying it in your personal style. Remember, self-confidence doesn't mean that you are overly outgoing or dominant. Often, self-confidence comes through very quietly yet strongly. Self-confidence will enhance effective communication because there is a lack of fear, which paves the way for open communication. A self-confident person has the courage to speak directly.

Have an Open-Door Policy

Establish an open-door policy from the beginning, inviting your cheerleaders to call you or meet with you privately if they have a concern. It's important for you to be approachable and to be able to build rapport with your squad members. Also remember to set guidelines regarding your availability so that squad members will not take advantage of your personal life. I recommend that you set off-limit times (except for emergencies) in the evening and weekends that are consistent with personal obligations.

Provide Appropriate Feedback

Praise in public and discipline in private. I have seen many cheerleaders mortified at being criticized in front of the group. Never embarrass or belittle anyone. If you need to give your cheerleaders constructive criticism in a specific area, then set up personal meetings. If you are in the habit of giving positive feedback in public, make sure you do not show inadvertent favoritism by lavishing a lot of attention on just a few people. Praise should be honest and deserved. Your cheerleaders may lose respect for you if you pour on unjustified praise.

Celebrate

Compliment and celebrate small and large accomplishments. I think it's important for

coaches and squads to have reasons to celebrate, so I recommend spontaneous, informal parties to provide an opportunity to say "thank you" and to reinforce the hard work. Your relationship with your squad will improve if you are the kind of coach who welcomes fun and celebration after a great performance or well-planned spirit event. The spontaneity of the celebration may provide an opportunity for your communication lines to open because of the festive mood and camaraderie.

FUN-AND-GAMES RELAY RACES

I have surprised my cheerleaders after practice with the Fun-and-Games Relay Races. After I divide them into two teams, we go outside and I explain the relays. The object is to be the first team to complete the relay. The first relay is called the Spinning Spirit Leaders. I have the two teams line up, placing a baseball bat about 30 feet away from each team (one baseball bat per team). The first player from each team runs to the baseball bat and puts his or her forehead on the top of the baseball bat. While keeping the bottom of the baseball bat on the ground, the player walks or runs around the baseball bat five times, keeping the forehead on top. Then the player drops the baseball bat and runs back to the next player on the team, who repeats the sequence. The first team to finish is the winner.

The second relay is called Pole Panic. Each team has a pole about three feet long. Two team members straddle the pole, one facing forward and one facing backward. Holding the pole with their hands (between their legs) they walk or run to a designated line and back, giving the pole to the next two team members. The first team to complete the cycle wins the relay.

The third relay is called Water Balloon Toss. The team splits in two, with half of the team members facing the other half of the team members, about six feet apart. Each team member on one side has a water balloon and will throw it to a partner. After the teams toss and catch the water balloon, the teams move back three more feet. The team who still has an intact water balloon at the end is the winner.

The cheerleaders had so much fun with the relays that they became a tradition and were requested every year.

Avoid Comparisons

Avoid comparing individuals on your squad. Each person needs to feel special and unique. Too often, one person's strength is compared to another person's weakness. Among themselves, cheerleaders commonly compare their own skills with the skills of other squad members, and you need to counter this tendency by only positively validating your cheerleaders. Cheerleaders need only to compare themselves with their own potential, not the achievements of other cheerleaders on their squad. If you compare individuals on your squad, you may block effective communication because of their perceiving you as ranking, judging, or embarrassing them.

Be Respectful

Treat your cheerleaders with respect by delivering an organized program that improves through continual feedback. Remember to practice the Golden Rule ("do unto others as you would have others do unto you") as your guiding foundation. Your cheerleaders will treat you the way you treat them. You are establishing the behavior standards by how you communicate with your cheerleaders. Give your feedback with respect, and respectfully request and receive feedback in return. Mutual respect will enhance mutual communication.

Remember that you will encounter many different types of cheerleaders. And you may adjust your communication style slightly to more effectively relate to each specific individual. For instance, if you know someone is sensitive about a specific trait or low-skill area, be patient and kind in discussing that topic. Always attempt to build them up with praise and gentle guidance, while serving as a positive role model. The foundation of your program rests on the quality of your communication and the consistency of your philosophy. You cannot be all things to all cheerleaders, but you can be yourself while communicating in a positive manner.

Communicating With School Faculty

In order for the faculty to support your program, it's important for them to understand that you place academics before activities, that you have established specific objectives for your program, and that you expect high behavior standards in the classroom. You want to form a good relationship with the faculty so that you can work together to help cheerleaders meet responsibilities to both cheering and classwork. Three suggestions that you can utilize to convince faculty of your commitment to academics, objectives, and behavior standards are grade and conduct checks, teacher evaluation forms, and special activities.

Grade and Conduct Checks

Send a form to each teacher at the end of each grading period and at least once in between grading periods to request an updated progress report and any pertinent comments regarding the student on your squad. Inform the faculty that you are available for consultation regarding grades and classroom conduct. Your interest and follow-up will help convince your faculty that you are serious about maintaining high academic and behavior standards on your squad. Some schools provide grade checks for athletics. If the grades of the cheerleaders are not checked, suggest to the athletic director that the cheerleaders be included in the athlete grade checks. Cheerleaders usually must maintain academic eligibility like all athletes.

Teacher Evaluation Forms

Many coaches use teacher evaluation forms before tryouts to receive feedback about people interested in cheerleader positions. These forms allow the faculty member to rate characteristics such as conduct, cooperation, attitude, dependability, and attendance. A sample form appears in chapter 5. Using these forms before tryouts gives the faculty members an opportunity to give you feedback and get involved with the cheerleader selection process (in many cases, these teacher evaluation forms are figured into the total points in cheerleader selection). These forms help you learn more about your cheerleaders, and also alert you to possible problem areas. You may want to meet with teachers personally if you have questions about their comments. Communication with teachers will help you build a stronger program because you are receiving feedback from an important source.

Special Activities

Another way to get the faculty to support your cheerleading program is to include teachers in the planning of pep assemblies and other special activities. Some faculty members may want to actually be involved in skits or class competitions, and some may want to help with posters, homecoming events, or spirit dress-up days. Ask some of your faculty members to help judge spirit competitions, plan a special door decoration contest, or wear school colors on game days. By getting teachers involved in special activities, you will help them learn more about the demands of spirit leadership. If a cheerleader begins to struggle academically or if a behavior problem occurs in class, perhaps teachers who have been working with you in spirit activities will let you know what's going on so you can deal with the situation.

Communicating With Sport Team Coaches

Since cheerleaders support the athletic teams, establishing open lines of communication with the team coaches is extremely important. I recommend that you meet with the sport team coaches periodically throughout the season to make sure that your cheerleaders are serving the program effectively. Some coaches do not see the value of spirit teams as a help to their sports program, so be sure to approach with great care. Also, the athletic director usually has final authority over such things as the use of facilities, purchases of equipment, and transportation. Your athletic director needs to be completely informed about all aspects of the program. Areas that I think you should discuss with the sport team coaches (and the athletic director if possible) include game rules, sportsmanship, game schedules, facilities, special performances, and spirit building.

Game Rules

After your squad is selected, ask the sport team coaches to meet with the cheerleaders to review the appropriate times to cheer and to clarify the game rules. Some sport team coaches will also have players demonstrate plays and referee calls so the cheerleaders will have a clearer understanding of how to support the team most effectively. Communicating about this in advance will help prepare your cheerleaders for game action cheering. If your squad does not understand the game thoroughly, they cannot effectively support the team and lead the crowd. Your squad will gain more respect if they respond to the game accurately and lead the crowd decisively.

Sportsmanship

Ask your coaches to help you explain the sportsmanship standards for your city, league, district, conference, or state. It's very important that your cheerleaders have a solid understanding of their role regarding good sportsmanship, and it should come from you with support from the team coaches. Communication about sportsmanship at the beginning of the season will enhance the effectiveness and responsibility of your program.

THE SPORTSMANSHIP CHEER

Two squads that cheered for archrival teams just happened to be at summer camp together. While at camp, the squads got to know each other better and also learned the words and motions to a Sportsmanship Cheer ("Athletes, unite! Give it your best, fight! Sportsmanship, you see—Number One Priority!"). After the basketball season began, the cheerleaders from these two schools decided to neutralize some of the animosity between their teams by performing the Sportsmanship Cheer together in the middle of the basketball court before the big game began.

The fans were very surprised to see the cheerleaders from both schools take the floor before the game. They seemed a little stunned at the words to the cheer. After the cheer, both sides of the gym applauded. The squads hugged each other and went to opposite sides of the gym, ready to cheer for their teams. In their hearts, they knew that they had taken one small step toward improving relations between the two schools.

Game Schedules

Meet with your sport team coaches to get the current game schedules and calendar of events. Discuss how your cheerleaders will support all of the sports programs. Communicating about this in advance will help organize and establish your transportation, performance, and spirit plans.

Facilities

Discuss sharing facilities for practices. For safety and liability reasons, cheerleaders need to have good practice facilities, the same as the sport teams. Communication about this in advance will establish the effectiveness and safety of your practices (as well as possibly avoid a lawsuit later).

Special Performances

Make sure that you discuss your plans for pep assemblies, homecoming, bus trips, and halftime performances with your sport team coaches. Always remember that your primary purpose is to provide leadership for the games. The extras need to be agreed upon, especially if you would like to include the coaches and some of the players in your plans. Communicating about this in advance will pave the way for a more effective season since spirit activities, performances, and bus trips all take thorough planning.

Spirit Building

If you would like to decorate the locker room or hallway lockers of individual players, check with the sport team coaches for approval. Do not take anything for granted. Always get approval for all plans in advance. Communicating about this in advance will enable you to delegate responsibility, plan thoroughly, and avoid potential conflicts.

You will want to establish open lines of communication with the sport team coaches as you develop your program because they can make your job much easier by working with you instead of against you. Communicate with them as often as you need and ask for feedback on how your cheerleaders augment their programs. Advance planning and direct communication will aid you in building an organized program.

Communicating With Parents

Building trust and rapport with the parents of your cheerleaders is extremely important.

Because of the time commitment and demands of cheerleading, parents want to feel assured that your program is fair, organized, and enriching. A lot of parents like to get involved in the activities of their child or teenager. Be sure to watch that the parents do not try to take too much of a hold on your program or become too involved: just be aware that this can happen and be prepared to handle it. Your job as cheerleading coach will run much smoother if you have the support of the parents. Here are some suggestions for building good communication with the parents of your cheerleaders before and after tryouts, at monthly meetings, and through mailings or reminders. The quality and frequency of that communication will determine your success with the parents.

Before and After Tryouts

Before tryouts, send home a pre-tryout packet outlining the expectations and requirements of your program that includes a permission form for the parents to sign. A sample of this form appears in chapter 5. By sending home all of this pre-tryout information, parents can understand and appreciate how your program is organized. You will establish a solid foundation for good parent relations by providing the information up-front.

After your squad is selected, have a meeting with the parents to discuss all aspects of your program and to answer questions. You may also want to consider asking parents to sign up to help on upcoming fundraising projects or special events that involve extra help (Homecoming float, pep rally that involves community members, or a bus trip that needs chaperons). This face-to-face meeting will enable the parents to ask you questions directly about your program, thus providing open access to information.

Monthly Meeting

If needed, set up a monthly meeting (in the evening) so that parents will have the opportunity to bring up issues, ask questions, or offer ideas. A monthly meeting will keep the lines of communication open and will help you gain cooperation during the year. Consider having it only if there are important issues to discuss.

Mailings or Reminders

One way to stay in contact with the parents of your cheerleaders is to mail a newsletter every month outlining upcoming events. The parents need to know what responsibilities they and their cheerleaders are expected to fulfill. If you do not want to mail a newsletter you can print up the information and send it home with your cheerleaders. Either way, keep your parents informed and offer to meet or speak with them if they need clarification or have concerns.

As you become better acquainted with the parents of your cheerleaders, you will gain insight on how to meet challenges if they occur. Open lines of communication that establish an honest, straightforward relationship from the very beginning of your program will allow more effective handling of problems when or if they occur. Almost all parents are interested in what you're doing, and some want to be involved with their student's activities.

Communicating With the Student Body

Communication with the student body will depend largely on the status of the cheerleading program and the participation of the individuals in that program. The reputation or status of the cheerleaders in your school will both influence and be influenced by the quality of the communication with the student body. The cheerleaders function as both members and representatives of the student body while at the same time fulfilling a role that sets them apart.

- As members of the student body they communicate with their own circle of friends and other students first of all as separate, individual students in the school.
- As representatives of the student body they wear a school uniform that communicates a certain position in the school and in the community, losing some of their individuality.
- As the link between the team and the crowd, they communicate on a different level with people (from one-to-one communication to a one-to-many level). They are expected to fulfill a special leadership role within the

school that sets them apart from other students.

I feel three things influence how successful a cheerleader will be when communicating with the student body. These three areas are the verbal communication skills (the actual words that are said and the organization of the message), the level of confidence (speaking with knowledge and authority), and the feeling of sincerity (honesty and consistency in word and action). The types of things that cheerleaders will communicate are information about upcoming games, pep rallies, fundraising programs, spirit contests, words to cheers and chants, and service projects.

As individuals and as a group, cheerleaders can improve communication with the student body by hanging up posters or handing out announcements about upcoming events. They can make announcements over the school's intercom system. They can ask different clubs and organizations to be involved in pep assemblies and hang up a Spirit News Bulletin Board in the main hallway of the school to serve as a communication center about school spirit activities. They can submit articles to the school newspaper that detail upcoming activities, make sportsmanship suggestions, show appreciation for individuals and groups who support school spirit, list words to cheers and chants, describe spirit day themes and service projects, and honor special faculty.

Individual cheerleaders can improve their communication with the student body by remembering the importance of honest leadership, exemplary behavior, and genuine friendship. The development of personal communication skills will enhance the quality of the communication, which hopefully will go beyond the mere exchange of information and toward the expression and development of caring individuals.

Here are some ideas on how to develop communication skills in your cheerleaders:

1. Rotate responsibilities and leadership opportunities. Your cheerleaders will benefit from the opportunity to gain firsthand experience in different roles.

2. Use praise and positive reinforcement to build self-confidence. Honest, immediate validation for the behavior you want to continue helps the cheerleader feel confident about doing a good job.

3. Make everyone feel important by listening, seeking feedback, and trying their ideas. By encouraging and reinforcing good communication skills in your cheerleaders, you will be able to enhance your overall program because you have helped your cheerleaders feel more confident about their leadership roles. They will begin to take more responsibility and contribute more to the program.

Communicating With Community Members

The cheerleaders are one of the most highly visible groups of student representatives in your school. They wear the uniforms, they stand out in front, they move, they make noise. Their job is to provide the leadership link between the fans and the players. Like most student organizations, the cheerleaders need the cooperation and support of the business people, the service organizations, and the clubs within the community. Cheerleaders need this cooperation because their job is not only to teach the message (of spirit and support) but to unify, direct, and deliver the message.

You can help the local community contribute to crowd control and sportsmanship by explaining how they can support the team through exemplary behavior. You can provide information to the local newspaper, the school paper, or in the printed sports program about sportsmanship, schedules of spirit events, and words to cheers and chants. Some schools also send a letter to the parents of all students about the upcoming sporting events, emphasizing the importance of good sportsmanship and positive behavior during games.

Members of the local community also determine the success of your fundraising projects. They provide financial support during the year by becoming involved in your plans. The quality of your publicity and advance communication about your financial needs will help your community understand why you require money for uniforms, camp, and supplies. One way to communicate these needs is to assemble a financial portfolio the way businesses do, listing your necessities, desires, and goals. Another way is to make a chart (such as a large thermometer) listing each item and how much it costs. As the money is generated, the area is colored in for a graphic representation of the success of the campaign.

The following is a list of suggestions on how to get more businesses and organizations involved with your program by inviting participation, communicating needs, interactive visiting, and expressing appreciation.

Invite

Have a Community Support Day as a theme for a pep assembly and invite representatives to be part of the activities. Give out special awards during the assembly to businesses and individuals who support the school. I have attended a Community Support Day pep rally where representatives from different businesses made floats, dressed up, and carried signs around the gym during the pep assembly. This event needs to be publicized extensively for greater involvement.

Communicate

Write articles for the local newspaper or send home letters with the students that communicate upcoming events and how people can get involved. Be sure to express appreciation for past support.

Visit

Personally visit businesses and organizations to invite them to be involved in a spirit week activity, Homecoming, or fundraising program. Keep updating your list of names, addresses, and phone numbers of those businesses and organizations that support your program. Offer to provide a mini-pep rally for employees or give a talk on school spirit and sportsmanship. Personal visits are a very effective way to promote your program.

Thank

Write thank you notes to individuals at businesses or organizations who have supported your program in any way.

As the cheerleading coach, you will want to provide the members of your community an opportunity to support the young leaders in your school while also supporting the athletic programs. Members of the community usually take great pride in their young people and usually want to support the activities: young leaders represent the future of the community. In order to secure community support, you need to remember the importance of publicity, personal communication in the form of letters or visits, and involvement in school activities. Since your cheerleaders are not only representatives from your school but also your community, your involvement with the local community will have an important impact on your total program.

Summary

These are the items that need to be considered when communicating your approach:

- The quality of your program is directly influenced by the quality of your communication with your cheerleaders, the faculty, the sport team coaches, the parents, the student body, and the local community.
- Establish a personal relationship with each cheerleader to enhance your level of communication.
- Cheerleaders learn more by what you do than by what you say.
- Honesty, positive attitude, self-confidence, and respect are important traits to remember when communicating with your cheerleaders.
- Rotate responsibilities or leadership opportunities among your cheerleaders, use positive reinforcement to build self-confidence, and be a good listener.

- Involving the faculty in your communications shows your commitment to academics.
- Meet with the sport team coaches to discuss game rules, sportsmanship, game schedules, facilities, special performances, and spirit building.
- To build trust and rapport with the parents of your cheerleaders, communicate with them before tryouts with an information packet, after tryouts with a meeting, and periodically with meetings and mailings.
- Cheerleaders and coaches can improve their communication with the student body with posters, handouts, announcements, and articles in the student newspaper.
- Cheerleaders need the cooperation and support of business people and service organizations within the community.
- To get more businesses and organizations involved with your program, invite them to participate in a pep assembly, write articles for the local newspaper inviting their participation, make personal visits to them, and thank them for their participation.

Chapter 3

© CLEO Photography

Motivating Cheerleaders

The practice right before the Homecoming pep rally was disastrous. One cheerleader fell when running out, timing on the jumps was off, the pyramid didn't go up, transitions were choppy, and personality projection was definitely lacking. You're worried, your squad is nervous, then . . . BOOM! The squad explodes onto the basketball court, jumps are perfect, the pyramid is strong and clean, transitions are smooth and exciting, and everyone beams with spirit. The crowd immediately jumps to its feet for a standing ovation. What motivated this dramatic change?

One of your greatest coaching challenges is motivating your cheerleaders. In this chapter, you will discover how to use principles of motivation to encourage your athletes to be the best they can be. I offer a number of suggestions for verbal and nonverbal reinforcement and goal setting, and discuss motivational concepts that apply to pride and tradition, coed cheering, and competition.

What Is Motivation?

Although motivation is very complex, I tend to think of it as the need or desire that causes a person to act, the level of which will vary from one cheerleader to another. If you're interested in learning more about motivation, you might read *Successful Coaching* or *Coaches Guide to Sport Psychology*, both written by Rainer Martens and published by Human Kinetics. Both books contain easy-to-use, detailed discussions of how coaches can apply scientific principles of motivation. My thoughts about motivation start with the belief that we can reinforce, validate, appreciate, compliment, suggest, teach, demand, encourage, and facilitate the behavior we desire from our cheerleaders, but we cannot regulate or predict their motivation.

It is important for each person on the squad to feel special. Avoid making comparisons among squad members. Individuals on your squad need to feel that you truly care, that you can be trusted, and that you will always treat everyone fairly. Nationally recognized motivational speaker Zig Ziglar has said that people don't care how much you know until they know how much you care. A solid foundation of care, trust, and fairness will help establish the basis for a genuine relationship. If your cheerleaders feel that you care about them, they are more likely to share their sources of motivation, leading to greater understanding on your part.

As you get to know your cheerleaders better, you will begin to understand what each person desires to "get out" of cheerleading. You will become familiar with individuals' personal motivation as you evaluate their development, contribution, and attitude. Many cheerleaders like to cheer because of the social interaction, the excitement, and the physical challenge of cheerleading. For some, expressing individuality through cheerleading is both risky and exhilarating. As coach of a multidimensional group with varying degrees of intrinsic and extrinsic motivation, you need to contemplate the sources of each individual's motivation in order to bring out the best in the group.

Motivation is one of the hardest parts of coaching cheerleaders. Different times of the year require different types of motivation. During summer practices your efforts will center around the back-to-school performance and wanting to make a good impression. As the football season gains momentum, Homecoming activities and achieving goals you set at the beginning of the season are in the forefront. Between seasons, you may need some new ideas to get everyone geared up for basketball. If attitudes and energy start to change for the worse as the year goes on, you can set fresh goals, focus on unity activities, and plan a special event. Keep in mind that motivation levels will vary from person to person and can take a roller coaster ride during the year.

Motivational Concepts

You can adapt the following basic concepts of motivation to the needs of your individual squads. Evaluate how each of the areas I discuss could help you develop your own program to motivate your cheerleaders.

Verbal Reinforcement

Reinforcement in cheerleading is a way to validate your cheerleaders. Positive feedback and individual attention will enhance their performance as a group. Verbal reinforcement consists of the words you use when you talk to your cheerleaders. You can't expect your cheerleaders to know how you feel about them or how everything is going unless you talk to them. Remember to use their names, be specific about what you are praising, and praise in front of everyone whenever possible. Don't embarrass or scold in front of others. One-on-one meetings will give you the opportunity to validate individuals, give (and receive) feedback, and listen for additional insights into their personal development.

Nonverbal Reinforcement

The spoken word is not always the most effective way to communicate. Nonverbal reinforcement is another way of connecting with your cheerleaders in an attempt to validate them.

One thing I like to do to encourage my cheerleaders is to help them prepare Discovery Notebooks that contain inspirational poems, quotations, and articles. Throughout the year, I bring handouts to practices and events so the cheerleaders can put them right into their notebooks. These handouts can pump up the spirit, turn up the volume, and fire-up the energy of your cheerleaders because they remind your squad members to look for the positive and focus on teamwork. Inspirational, positive literature can help build good attitudes, a feeling of optimism, and provide nonverbal reinforcement for hard work.

I hug a lot. If you are comfortable hugging people, even if you don't know them very well, I highly recommend it. I believe that people like to be hugged, whether they will admit it or not. I feel that hugging serves as a source of motivation for cheerleaders because the hug represents a form of affection and validation, two basic human needs. There are many times when words are not necessary or can get in the way. Hugging your cheerleaders is a great way to both start and end a practice. However, coaches need to be sensitive to squad members who don't want to be hugged. Hugs taken without permission are not a good idea. Use your own discretion.

If giving and receiving hugs is too difficult for you, or if you have squad members who don't like to be hugged, then you can give nonverbal reinforcement by being a good listener. Knowing when someone needs silent attention is very important to the development of a relationship. You can sometimes tell if a cheerleader needs this by noticing body language. They may seem to either "hang around" or withdraw from the group.

Writing appreciation notes or giving spirit presents (a small gift, such as a button, that represents a special feeling or slogan) are other forms of nonverbal reinforcement. I have also used a set of brightly colored signs that say WOW, SUPER, SENSATIONAL, FANTASTIC, TERRIFIC, and YES. If I am sitting across the gym, for instance, I can hold up signs to convey my approval when the cheerleaders are doing a great job during a game. This is a fun way to send a nonverbal message. Also, remember to have a smile handy during practices and games for sending positive messages to your cheerleaders.

A hug, a smile, a note, a sign, or simply silent attention can all send nonverbal reinforcement to your cheerleaders. Your thoughtfulness will help cultivate their inner motivation to do their best and be their best.

WORDS OF ENCOURAGEMENT

After I had been coaching cheerleaders for many years, I was asked by the University of Missouri, Kansas City, to start a coed cheerleading program for their new basketball team. After selecting the squad, I was busy helping them prepare for their first preseason performance. On the evening of the big event, I was worried and excited at the same time. I wasn't sure how everything would turn out, but I wanted to be prepared.

I made some signs about one-fourth the size of a regular piece of posterboard and put brightly colored, motivational words on them such as WOW, TERRIFIC, SUPER, and GREAT. I was seated across the gym from my squad, on a lower row so they could see me. I clutched my signs and hoped for the best as my squad exploded onto the floor with spirit and energy. I'm very happy to report that my new collegiate squad did an outstanding job that night, and as they left the basketball court they looked over at me with beaming faces. I was so proud of them, and I let my signs do the talking from across the gym.

Goal Setting

Because people are motivated to achieve goals that are important to them, I like my cheerleaders to set individual and squad goals. For individual goals I have them list cheering and personal improvement goals, and for squad goals they list skill, unity, and school spirit goals. I will explain each area step by step.

Individual Cheer Goals

Most cheerleaders know what cheering skills they need to work on. If yours need help deciding which skills to work on, you may want to have a meeting with each individual to discuss your impressions from tryouts, observations from early practices, or the results of a Skill Sheet (which is explained in chapter 5). The cheerleader first lists the area of needed improvement, such as jumps, followed by the specific goal, such as "My toe touch jump will meet excellent performance standards as established by the coach in time for the Homecoming pep rally." The next step is to set up a plan or a commitment to achieve the goal. In this case, the cheerleader would list what conditioning and strengthening program would be used to improve the toe touch jump.

Your role in this goal-setting exercise is to help your cheerleader select goals that are achievable and that are important to both the individual and to the squad. The goal should be stated specifically with a target date for successful completion. Also, make sure that you approve the plan for achieving the goal, checking for safety, physical demands, time restraints, and practicality.

© Thomas J. Benincas, Jr.

Personal Improvement Goals

The next step in helping your cheerleaders set goals is to ask them to evaluate their own personality and decide on an improvement area that would contribute to teamwork and friendship on the squad. Some cheerleaders decide their personal improvement goal would be to have more patience when things don't run smoothly or to be more thoughtful about the feelings of others. The goal of "patience," stated more clearly, could be something like this: "I will be more patient with the captain during practices by not complaining, by not making a face, and by giving 100 percent effort. I will remain poised and positive when times get rough." "Thoughtfulness" could be clarified this way: "I will really listen when someone is talking and try to understand that person. I will share a kind word, give a hug, or send a note to someone who needs a little lift." The plan or commitment to achieve the goal requires listing circumstances where these traits are needed and preparing mentally to respond with the appropriate behavior.

Squad Skill Goals

Meet with your cheerleaders to discuss squad goals. Most coaches and squads know what areas need work by evaluating the skill levels during tryouts and paying attention to what's been happening at practices. To help your squad set squad skill goals, collect information from informal evaluations during practice, videos you may have taken during performances, and visions of what your squad members want to look like.

You can also help your cheerleaders set squad skill goals by isolating specific upcoming challenges (such as a commitment to a competition, a special performance for Homecoming, or an exhibition at a local elementary school). Your squad will only be motivated to achieve goals that are important to them, and you may need to guide them in selecting goals that are desirable, attainable, and challenging.

Examples of squad skill goals would be improving dance skills for an upcoming performance, working on more precise arm motions, adding perfect toe touches to a cheer, or working on more effective voices (pitch, expression, and enunciation). For instance, if your squad wants to work on more precise arm motions, your plan may include a specific time during practice to work only on arm motions, to use videotape to visually observe the progress, or to ask a college cheerleader or private coach to come over to help develop better arm motions. After these goals are listed, discuss your plan or commitment to achieve the goals with the squad. Remember to decide on a target date for completion.

Squad Unity Goals

Building squad unity and friendship will help keep your program focused and fun. Squad cohesiveness is discussed in chapter 4, which will give you many ideas for establishing squad unity. Most squads set unity goals that center around being patient with each other, making a commitment to building friendships on the squad, being supportive of individual effort and accomplishment, and encouraging teamwork with a spirit of cooperation.

After the unity goals are selected, you need to talk about how issues that interfere with squad unity will be handled: for example, how to prevent long practices from affecting moods or focus, how to counteract talking behind someone's back, bad attitudes that crop up, or disagreements with squad leaders. By reviewing issues that disrupt unity, squad members can begin to understand how much individual effort and commitment are needed to achieve squad unity goals.

School Spirit Goals

Building school spirit is one of the primary responsibilities facing your cheerleaders. As the coach, you can improve the quality of the commitment and the depth of their motivation by helping them set school spirit

Squad Goals

Skill

1.
2.
3.

Unity

1.
2.
3.

Spirit

1.
2.
3.

Individual Goals

Name	***Skill Goals***	***Personal Goals*** (attitude, communication, or leadership goals)
Megan		
Ray		
Laura		
Gary		
Lisa		
Dale		
Linda Lee		
Chad		
Ashley		
Andy		
Gina		
Burt		

Figure 3.1 Goal board example.

goals. First, talk about school spirit and ask what they want to do to promote it during the upcoming season. Examples of school spirit goals might include improving crowd involvement during the games by trying new crowd techniques, planning an extra special Homecoming activity, making more posters or banners to decorate the school, sending appreciation notes to faculty members who support the cheerleaders, giving out a Spirit Questionnaire to find out how students think school spirit can be improved, or making spirit gifts for individual sport team players. Numerous school spirit ideas are listed in chapter 10 in case you need help deciding which goals to set for your program and school. After these goals are listed, have your cheerleaders specify what they will do each week to improve school spirit.

I like to put all of the goals on a posterboard so the squad can review them regularly. Reviewing the goals will help keep your squad focused and remind them of what has been established for the success of the entire program. Figure 3.1 provides an example of how to set up a goal board.

Squad and Personal Fitness Goals

Besides setting individual and squad goals, it's important for your cheerleaders to make a commitment to physical fitness and optimum health. Here are some ways you can encourage a lifetime commitment to goals in those areas:

1. Periodically give out articles on nutrition and eating disorders, fitness, and health.
2. Set up specific times each week when the squad walks or jogs together.
3. Work out in the school's weight room, go to a health spa, or work out at a local gym. Note that working out at a health spa or local gym as a team may be against school policy for liability reasons—check this out first.
4. Set up a regular aerobics class.
5. Establish a tradition of and commitment to a program free of alcohol, tobacco, or other drugs.
6. Encourage your cheerleaders to be good role models and to volunteer for community fitness and health events.
7. Give out special recognition awards validating hard work and commitment.

As the coach of athletes who are cheerleaders, one of the benefits you can offer squad members in your program is an appreciation for health and fitness. You can teach them that they are responsible as individuals for the quality of their health experience in life but that it is something that they can also work toward as a group. One of the important benefits that cheerleaders experience, sometimes without being aware of it, is the exhilaration of feeling strong, powerful, and healthy. This feeling can serve as a dominant motivator for their involvement in and commitment to your athletic program.

Pride and Tradition

An important source of motivation for your cheerleaders is pride. Developing a program you can be proud of may take a few years, but the benefits are multiple. Your cheerleaders need to feel good about wearing the school uniform and representing the program. A side benefit of being associated with a student leadership group within the school is a sense of identity. Cheerleaders will identify with each other and with the philosophy and structure of your program. The intensity of their pride will help determine the quality and success of your program.

Here are some of the benefits of developing a program that you are proud of:

- Development of your own character and self-esteem
- Respect in the community for you personally and for your program
- Deeper commitment from parents and cheerleaders who want to be associated with your program
- Cooperation from faculty and students in building school spirit

WELCOME HOME

The band was playing, people were gathering, and the spirit was soaring. The small town was celebrating a huge victory. My friend's squad had won first place at the state cheerleading competition and, upon returning home, was surprised by the festivities of proud friends, family members, and community leaders. The spotlight usually reserved for a football or basketball team was now shining brightly on a cheerleading squad. When my friend called me with the exciting details of that glorious homecoming, I could feel her emotion and gratitude when she said, "My squad has worked so hard and has never received appreciation. They will never forget the huge banner that hung at our party: 'Welcome home, State Champs! We are proud of you!'"

One way to help develop pride among your cheerleaders is to speak only in positive terms about your squad to others. For instance, brag about your squad to other coaches and faculty members in front of the squad. And if your cheerleaders are involved in a school or community service project, make sure that the squad receives recognition from others, such as over the school intercom system or in the school newspaper. Be sure to validate individuals who go the extra mile and bring attention to the squad with service or spirit activities.

Another way to build pride into the squad's identity is to strictly enforce the behavior standards of written rules and regulations or your cheerleader constitution. Chapter 4 discusses the tasks of developing rules and regulations and writing a cheerleader constitution (see Appendix A for a model constitution). A constitution usually details philosophy, guidelines, and practical information, as well as appearance standards for uniforms and grooming so that your cheerleaders will set a positive example. Your cheerleaders will develop pride in your program because they are living up to the high expectations placed on them.

Tradition plays an important role in the group's motivation, cohesion, and identity. Traditional events bind the squads to each other and to the squads that have gone before them. Some coaches and cheerleaders look forward to these traditional events because they are fun and serve as a reward for days, weeks, and months of hard work.

Many squads develop traditions participating in some of the following areas:

- Pre-tryout training sessions conducted by outgoing seniors
- Initiation, party, or early morning breakfast for new members
- Annual holiday party
- Involvement with pep pals, little sisters or brothers, or secret pals for gift exchange and encouragement during the year
- Special community cheer clinic for younger children
- Homecoming event (such as slumber party)
- Lock-in at the school to work on cheers, chants, posters, and banners
- Awards banquet
- Picnic or summer swim party
- Involvement in local service project or charity event

THE LAUGHTER AND THE TEARS

It was time for our end-of-the-year banquet and we were discussing what we should do. I suggested making some changes in our usual format, but my cheerleaders wanted us to continue the traditions that had formed many years earlier. The night of the banquet is always very special. We invite the families to share our festivities.

After the dinner, we have the program. First, the graduating seniors put on a skit for everyone, capturing the funnier moments that happened during the year. Then I announce the winners of the squad votes for Most Improved, Most Inspirational, Best Athlete, Most Spirited, Outstanding Leadership, and Most Likely to Cheer in College. The last activity of the banquet is the slide show, consisting of faces, places, and happenings of our year. The background music features the sentimental songs that were popular during our time together. The annual banquet begins as a festive party and ends with the laughter and tears of special memories.

Traditions are formed in many different ways. Sometimes a coach will initiate an event that turns out to be very popular and squads will continue the tradition each year. Other times a tradition will form from an idea learned at a cheerleading camp or from another squad. Sometimes a tradition will evolve from a tragedy. For instance, I know of a school who performs the same dance every year to commemorate a squad member who died during her senior year. The routine was her favorite.

The traditions sustained by your squads will continue to enhance pride, unity, and spirit throughout the year because they provide a flow of experience, memories that link individuals to a history, and motivation to share in the joy of community.

Coed Cheerleading

Quite a few cheerleading coaches have reported to me that adding males to their program helped motivate the females that were already on the squad. Adding males to a previously all-female squad changes the appearance, the performance, and the dynamics of the squad. Visually, coed squads are usually larger in size. With the increased number of cheerleaders, the squads also have the opportunity to perform pyramids and advanced stunts. These extra dimensions serve as powerful motivators to hard-working squads because the possibilities for high-level performance are usually increased.

A small but growing percentage of high schools have developed coed cheerleading over the past few years. The high visibility of coed college and university squads, coupled with televised cheer competitions, has sparked the involvement of males in cheerleading. Adding males to your squad may not be easy because of existing attitudes (since cheerleading appears to be dominated by females, some males are resistant to being involved). Here's how some schools have successfully recruited males to their cheerleading program:

1. The cheerleading coach at the school is a former male collegiate cheerleader and can recruit guys to the program.
2. The females on the squad have male friends who were recruited to attend some practices to assist with partner stunts and pyramids for an upcoming event.
3. Males that are involved in other sports (for instance, wrestling, football, and basketball) are recruited to the squad during their off-season.
4. A male gymnastics coach encourages males to contribute their talents to the cheerleading program.
5. Males who are involved in student government (and spirit activities) can sometimes be recruited to the cheerleading program because they are rowdy during games and are natural leaders.
6. A professional male instructor from a national cheerleading organization can conduct a clinic for males who are interested in learning how to perform partner stunts and build pyramids.
7. A male school mascot may decide he would rather cheer with the squad than wear a costume.

When recruiting males to join your program, look for those who are athletic, have a good attitude, and are responsible, confident, and secure (some males are ridiculed for their cheerleading involvement). An outgoing, rowdy personality is an added plus. Role models for males in your program may be found on other coed squads in your area, on videos of coed cheerleading competitions, at clinics and camps, and on collegiate squads.

Most males will be very excited about learning partner stunts and pyramids because these skills are very athletic. Some males resist arm motions because they don't want to risk doing anything that may appear effeminate. Be patient. Male college cheerleaders are excellent role models for athletic arm motions.

Males benefit from cheerleading because it is another opportunity to develop athletic skills. A lot of male high school and college cheerleaders are former football players, wrestlers, and basketball players who, for many different reasons, decided to try cheerleading. These males get to remain involved in sports, develop fitness habits, and experience the fun of cheering all at the same time. Coed cheerleading can be a fun, challenging, and rewarding source of motivation for your program. It can also provide a powerful impact on school spirit.

Cheer Competitions

Competition for cheerleaders has gained popularity over the past decade due to national cheerleading companies hosting competitions and to televised coverage of high school and collegiate cheer competitions. Cheer competitions are often a major source of motivation for cheerleaders because they enjoy the challenge of shifting gears from a supportive role to a competitive role. As a coach, you have probably already decided if competition is good for your program or not. Hopefully, chapter 1 helped you establish your objectives and evaluate if competition is appropriate for your squad. In chapter 11, I discuss the issue of whether cheerleaders should compete or not, provide a list of different types of competitions, and give you information on how to prepare mentally and physically for a competition. Competition serves as a powerful source of motivation for many cheerleaders, so be sure to get feedback from your squad about this decision.

Summary

Here are the key points about motivating cheerleaders:

- Motivation is the need or desire that causes a person to act.
- Your job as coach includes understanding each cheerleader's personal motivation and helping individuals meet internal needs.
- Verbal reinforcement, such as public praising, is an important source of motivation for your cheerleaders.
- Inspirational, positive literature can help motivate your cheerleaders to build good attitudes and a feeling of optimism.
- A hug, a smile, a note, a sign, or simply silent attention are all ways to send nonverbal reinforcement to your cheerleaders.
- People are motivated to achieve goals that are important to them. Have sessions with your cheerleaders to set individual skill goals and personal improvement goals.
- Have a squad meeting to set squad goals for developing skill, improving unity, and boosting school spirit.
- Besides setting individual and squad goals, it is important for your cheerleaders to make a commitment to physical fitness and optimum health. For instance, give out articles on nutrition, fitness, and health, set up a regular aerobics class, and establish a commitment to a program that's free of alcohol, tobacco, and other drugs.
- Pride is an important source of motivation for your cheerleaders because of the identification with a positive program of esteem, service, and high standards.
- Tradition, as a source of motivation, binds the squads to each other as individuals and to the squads who have gone before.
- Adding males to a previously all-female squad changes the appearance, performance, motivation, goals, and dynamics of the squad.
- Many schools have been successful in adding males to their cheerleading program by recruiting males involved in other sports, enlisting the help of a male college cheerleader or professional instructor, or hiring a male coach who is a former college cheerleader.
- Cheer competitions can serve as a source of motivation for your cheerleaders.

Chapter 4

© National Cheerleaders Association 1996

Building a Cheerleading Program

Building a cheerleading program means assembling the components of experience that will ultimately define what makes your program unique. To me, building is the same thing as growing: You learn from mistakes, try new ideas, and reach for the next level of success. Building a program takes time, energy, knowledge, and care. It requires a structure that is solid enough to endure change and flexible enough to encompass change. Each day with your cheerleaders offers opportunities for you to improve your process. How your program unfolds is a decision both you and your squad make: "This is the way we do things . . . this is the way we'll work together."

I will focus on six key components of building a program:

- Building unity
- Building leadership
- Sportsmanship and school spirit responsibilities
- Fundraising
- Public relations and service
- Discipline and rules

Select the ideas and examples that you think will work best for you. You can build a supreme program by considering all the options.

Building Unity

Squad cohesiveness is the heart of your program. By incorporating squad unity activities into your program structure, you create bonds of friendship and camaraderie that pervade the practices and performances. If your cheerleaders enjoy sharing time together as friends, they will be more likely to work harder, which will help keep the program running smoothly. To be an effective squad, everyone must feel a sense of "common unity" or community. The act of serving as a squad member does not automatically bring unity to the squad: Special times together are essential to unite individuals for a common goal.

There are many things you can do to contribute to your squad's unity. The following ideas can be used once a week, once a season, or once a year. Evaluate each one in light of your own personal style and the needs of your squad.

Ideas for Building Squad Unity

Goal Setting

Once a week, take time to set individual and squad goals. Also, try to do at least one unity-building session per week, conducted either by you or by one of your squad members. Chapter 3 discusses additional goal-setting strategies.

Thank You Notes

Squad members will often help each other with both cheerleading and noncheerleading activities. I feel it's important to take time to thank each other and share an appreciation for the individual leadership qualities, thoughtfulness, and skill development that contribute to the success of the squad. Pass out store-bought thank you notes or create your own on a personal computer. Have each squad member write and deliver a thank you note to a designated person on the squad (either assign people, draw names, or choose the person sitting on the right or left) and share the results with each other.

Appreciation Cards

Give each squad member index cards with the names of individual cheerleaders on them. Have every member write a short, personal appreciation on each card. After the cards are distributed, each squad member can select one to share with the group.

Picnic Practice

Plan a practice in a park and ask each person to bring food, plus an original cheer or chant to share. Spend some time working on new cheers and chants after everyone has shared. This is a great exercise for mid-season slump. This idea can also be done with a slumber party or pizza party.

Pillow Cases

Each person brings a white pillow case and a few permanent markers. Squad members write and draw on each other's pillow cases. The pillow cases can then be used on a pillow or hung in a bedroom as a memento.

Quote of the Day

Squad members take turns bringing a poem or positive quote to practice. Share it at the beginning of practice or at the end as a closing.

Squad Diary or Scrapbook

Every time your squad gets together (practices, games, special events) write something in a diary or scrapbook. Add photographs during the year. Collect "famous last words" from squad members and capture the essence of your squad by what is written.

Videotape

Have someone videotape your squad at practices, pep rallies, games, and other special events. Put it all together and show at mid-season or end of the year. If possible, make a copy for each person on the squad.

The Birth of Spirit

Each squad member brings a baby picture and puts it on a posterboard or bulletin board. Then have everyone guess which cheerleader is what baby. To carry the theme further, have a crawling relay, have a baby bottle drinking contest, and serve baby food for snacks.

Secret Pal

Have secret pals for a week, a month, or a season. You can either assign secret pals or have the squad members draw names. Each squad member builds the spirit of his or her secret pal by leaving notes, small gifts, or locker posters.

Hug Circle

End each practice with a hug circle. Have everyone lock arms in a circle, share funny or serious thoughts, make final announcements, and then lean into the circle for a very tight hug.

Y.E.S. Board

Y.E.S. stands for You're Extra Special. You can make a bulletin board or large posterboard with decorations. Use it to leave messages, notes, positive slogans, appreciations, thank yous, and schedules of upcoming events. This Y.E.S. Board can help build communication, unity, and spirit.

Personal Collage

Have squad members bring in old magazines, catalogs, scissors, glue, and a spiral notebook. Everybody cuts out pictures and slogans that represent themselves, glues them to the notebook cover, and makes minicollages to share with the group.

Rowdy Routine

Every squad member makes up one eight-count for a dance routine. Put it all together to music for a very rowdy dance routine.

Sweatshirt Exchange

Have the squad members draw names. At the next practice, they should bring a favorite sweatshirt to give to the person whose name they drew. Have them share why they selected this particular sweatshirt for that person. Decide if the sweatshirt is to be returned in a week, or if it is a gift.

Holiday Party

Have an annual holiday party with squad members drawing names and exchanging gifts.

Squad Song

Squad members come up with ideas for a squad song that will represent them for the year. The song is played as background music at the end of practice, at a slumber party, or during an awards banquet, or it can be sung on bus trips. It is usually a popular song that has special meaning for the squad.

© CLEO Photography

Squad Shield

The squad shield gives your squad members the opportunity to express who they really are, improve communication, set goals, and build unity. It can be made during the summer or at the beginning of each season and should be kept in a location where members can see it often to remind them of goals and appreciations.

Materials: a piece of posterboard and any other art materials you would like (markers, construction paper, glue, pictures from magazines, etc.)

Directions:

1. Draw a framework for the shield that is meaningful to your squad.
2. Divide the framework into five distinct areas.
3. Answer the following questions in the appropriate areas.

Contents:

1. List one characteristic everyone on the squad appreciates for each person.
2. List personal goals for each person on the squad to work on during the season.
3. Draw or cut out pictures illustrating three goals for this season.
4. Draw or cut out a picture illustrating your squad's most outstanding feature.
5. List three words you hope your student body will use to describe your squad this year.

Feedback Sheet

The following are questions you could use on a feedback sheet that can be given out at the end of each week to help improve communication, learn from past mistakes, set new goals, enhance self-awareness, and build squad unity.

Name of Cheerleader:

____

One Word That Describes This Week:

____

1. What is your overall feeling about how the squad functioned this week?
2. What is your overall feeling about how effective you were this week?
3. What areas could we have improved on?
4. What are specific problems or areas of dissension?
5. What is something special that happened to you this week?
6. What was your favorite part of the week?
7. What received the greatest response?
8. What was the most fun you had all week?
9. What new ideas made us more effective this week?
10. What are your personal goals for next week?
11. What areas do you think we should cover in our squad goals next week?
12. Do you have any general comments or insights?

Getting to Know You

The following exercise is a good way to introduce individuals to the group, learn more about people who are already familiar, and share something special about each other. As your squad members get to know one another, your squad cohesiveness will be enhanced. First, pair up and spend five to ten minutes talking. Take notes on what the other person says in response to the following list of things. Afterward, one person introduces the other, or each person shares individually.

- Share a nickname.
- Describe yourself in three words.
- Share a short-term or long-term goal.
- What would you like to be doing in 10 years?
- If you wrote a book today, what would the title be?
- What would you do if you had a magic wand?
- If you could become invisible, where would you like to go?
- Share a personal motto you live by.
- If you were required to donate six months to serving your community, state, or nation, what would you choose to do and why?

THE Y.E.S. BOARD

Throughout many years of working with cheerleaders, one of my favorite things to do is to put up a huge Y.E.S. Board. The Y.E.S. stands for You're Extra Special. Cheerleaders write appreciations, words of encouragement, positive affirmations, and thank yous on a huge posterboard or banner paper covering a wall. They may draw pictures on it and decorate it, too. The Y.E.S. Board becomes a communication and squad unity center as everyone writes on it throughout the year. At the end of the year, the contributions and artwork are cut apart and placed in a scrapbook. The reason I love the Y.E.S. Board so much is that to me it represents having a positive attitude toward life. Each day I can ask myself, "What will I write on the Y.E.S. Board of my life today?"

Building Leadership

Student leadership skills developed through various activities and responsibilities carried out by squad members provide your squad, as well as the school, with direction, vision, and commitment. These experiences lay a good foundation for individuals in their personal lives, contribute to the school climate, and enhance the effectiveness of your program from year to year.

The cheerleaders involved in your program have the opportunity to develop their leadership capacity because of the challenges and experiences that are built into your program. Each small success helps them develop confidence for future responsibilities. Your program will grow stronger as your cheerleaders gain experience, awareness, and expertise.

Developing Leadership Skills

Building your program and building leadership can occur at the same time because of the richness and progression of experience. For instance, if you rotate your captain or head cheerleader periodically, your squad members will be able to take turns experiencing the challenge of the position and the dynamics of leading and following. Another way to build your program through leadership enhancement is to rotate responsibilities periodically (weekly, biweekly, or monthly) so that squad members have the opportunity to handle different positions, such as co-captain, fundraising coordinator, or pep rally planner.

Creativity sessions can also build leadership. Have squad members break into small groups to work on new cheers, chants, dances, and pep rally skits they make up on the spot. Then have them present their ideas to the whole squad. Besides generating pep rally ideas, this will build confidence in fast thinking and in crowd leadership abilities.

Your cheerleaders can take an active leadership role in the school by forming a Spirit Council that promotes good sportsmanship, helps plan all pep rallies, and builds school spirit with Spirit Week activities. Besides squad members, the Spirit Council can be made up of representatives from Student Council, athletic team coaches, team captains, faculty members, and class officers. As you and your cheerleaders receive input from different interest groups, you will have more ideas to work with and your squad will gain valuable experience in listening, prioritizing, and building consensus.

Following are eight leadership development areas that will foster the leadership potential of individuals on your squad.

Goal Setting

If your program involves setting individual and squad goals, your cheerleaders will learn the importance of goals and techniques for setting long- and short-term goals. This important skill can make a positive impact on other aspects of your cheerleaders' lives.

Organization

Your cheerleaders will be involved in organizing Homecoming activities, halftime activities, pep rallies, spirit building, and other programs within your school. Their participation will provide them with opportunities to take responsibility for the follow-through in planning and conducting events for the school. These experiences help build leadership skills that will both augment and transcend your program.

Group Process

As the coach, you will be conducting many group activities as part of your program. Because of the involvement of your cheerleaders in activities such as unity-building experiences, your squad members will learn to observe and understand behavior. They will experience both cooperation and competition among squad members, see conflict management in action, and learn about the balance between individual and group concerns.

Problem Solving and Decision Making

Your squad will be making group decisions, thus giving them the opportunity to work through problems and to implement solutions. They will learn about styles of leadership and how to work together toward consensus.

Evaluation

As you evaluate your squad members' cheerleading and leadership skills, and they evaluate each other, they will learn about the process of evaluation as individuals and as a group.

Communication

Your use of verbal and nonverbal reinforcement, effective listening, and the quality of your interpersonal communication will facilitate the development of leadership traits in your cheerleaders.

Self-Awareness

Many of your activities will help build the self-esteem and personal motivation of your cheerleaders, both of which are essential in the development of leadership skills. For instance, mastering a specific skill area (such as a difficult jump or stunt) or receiving positive feedback on a personal trait help foster positive self-esteem as well as promote motivation.

Uniting Various Clubs

Another way to build leadership in your cheerleaders is to help them get all school clubs involved in effective leadership activities. Here are some suggestions for how to unite various clubs to promote school spirit and pride:

1. Hold monthly meetings of club presidents.
2. Start a fundraising calendar.
3. Make an all-school activities calendar.
4. Set up an activities bulletin board.
5. Start a Club Hall of Fame to validate achievements.
6. Plan an all-school project, such as a community clean up, National Club Week, or student visitation to neighboring schools.
7. Organize a P.R.I.D.E. Club (People Really Involved Doing Everything).
8. Get clubs involved in pep rallies, school assemblies, and crowd participation at games.

Encouraging a Commitment to Leadership

One way to develop leadership on your squad is to help establish a mindset about what it means to make a commitment to be a leader in the school. I have written a Leader's Code that highlights qualities of leadership that you may want your cheerleaders to understand and embody. The code includes 10 affirmations, each followed by a description.

THE LEADER'S CODE

by Linda Rae Chappell

I am honest.
I communicate the truth in my words and actions.

I am responsible.
I am a person of my word. I am dependable and sincere.

I am positive.
I have a good attitude. I approach each challenge with confidence.

I am fair.
I treat individuals equally, patiently, and respectfully.

I am dedicated.
I work hard for what I believe in. I set goals and achieve them.

I am patient.
I have time to listen to others. I try to understand people and situations as thoroughly as possible.

I am kind.
I take time to be a friend, give a hug, show I care.

I am energetic.
I set a good example by approaching situations enthusiastically. I go the extra mile.

I am respectful.
I am sensitive to the feelings of others. I treat individuals sincerely, consistently, seriously.

I am creative.
I am not afraid to take chances with new ideas. I am spontaneous, flexible, innovative.

Leadership training will be an ongoing challenge as you coach your squad(s). If you are committed to "building people through cheerleading," then it will be one of the most important aspects of your program.

Sportsmanship and School Spirit Responsibilities

It is very important to implement ideas in your program that help promote good sportsmanship and school spirit. Cheerleaders help "set the pace" regarding good conduct during sporting events and general support for the entire school. These components are important to your program because they help build spirit traditions in the school and can establish a carry-over from year to year.

Promoting Sportsmanship and School Spirit

Specific activities initiated by you and your cheerleaders can make a positive impact in your school. Since good sportsmanship and school spirit are two key responsibilities facing your cheerleaders, it is important that your program reflects your commitment to serving the school through positive activities. Here are some ideas of how to promote good sportsmanship and school spirit.

S.P.I.R.I.T. Club

Your cheerleaders can organize a S.P.I.R.I.T. Club (Student Pride Includes Real Involvement Together) to raise and support school spirit, good sportsmanship, and school and community pride.

Sportsmanship Clinic

Cheerleaders in a community, city, league, conference, district, or county can meet to have a special clinic featuring coaches, motivational speakers, and professional cheerleading instructors to discuss and demonstrate game rules, crowd involvement techniques, and sportsmanship guidelines. Standardize a cheer for opposing cheerleaders to perform together that sets the tone for sportsmanship at the beginning of the game. Form small groups of cheerleaders from different squads to discuss concerns, problems, and ideas. Share unity and communication exercises and establish pregame procedures and behavior standards of excellence.

Spirit News

Cheerleaders can present a weekly article for the school newspaper thanking students, faculty, and parents for their support at the games. Give recognition to individuals who are good role models and who exemplify the highest sportsmanship standards.

Sportsmanship Trophies or Awards

Cheerleaders (with help from teachers and other student organizations) can give special recognition to individuals or groups who contribute to the development of good sportsmanship. This can be set up on a point system where daily or weekly events all contribute to the final tally, or designated judges can observe every event and place votes at the end of each season.

Good Role Models

You will need to remind your cheerleaders that they are role models for other students in their school, middle school or junior high and elementary students, alumni, and the community in general. Good sportsmanship is good citizenship: the Golden Rule in action. Cheerleaders must not lead negative cheers, wave arms during free throws, stomp on the floor when opposing players are getting ready to serve in volleyball or take a free throw in basketball, or anything else that displays poor sportsmanship.

Game Rules

Make sure your cheerleaders know and understand all game rules in order to respond appropriately to the game situations. You might want to have a Rules Clinic with your school's coaches to go over game rules, situations, officials' calls, and sports protocol. Players can demonstrate and discuss important issues. Good communication can be established at this time.

Good Working Relationships

Your cheerleaders should establish good communication with the faculty, business community, parents, alumni, Booster Club, Pep Club, coaches, and players. Everyone working together (for instance, on a Spirit Council) will promote good sportsmanship and positive support.

Working With Other Students

If a student group at your school starts to develop a reputation for being rowdy or disruptive, have your cheerleaders meet with them to discuss options. This student group could be taught some special chants (to be led by the cheerleaders) or involved in a pep rally. Try to show these students positive ways to respond at games with your sportsmanship and spirit program.

Questionnaire

Have your cheerleaders compile a Spirit Questionnaire for your school's students to find out what cheers or chants they like, what traditions they will support, and what new ideas they may have regarding sportsmanship and student involvement.

Involvement of Elementary School Children

Your cheerleaders can conduct clinics for elementary (and junior high or middle school) students, teaching them simple cheers and chants to get them ready for the game. Have a special seating section for them. Be sure to discuss appropriate behavior before, during, and after the game. If possible, have something special for them: a T-shirt, minimegaphone, minipompons, or crowd involvement signs.

Leadership and Communication Skills

Your cheerleaders need good leadership and communication skills in order to promote and exemplify good sportsmanship. They must be assertive and confident in order to involve and excite the crowd. Cheerleaders need to be able to work with their peers and direct their energies away from actions inappropriate for athletic events. Cheerleaders cannot ignore negative behavior; they need to take a leadership stand and deal with circumstances in a firm and positive manner.

Posters and Pin-Ons

Your cheerleaders (with help from other students) can display sportsmanship-related posters and pin-ons to make students aware of school policy and standards of conduct. It is important to take a firm stand for positive behavior in your school.

Sportsmanship Theme for the Year

At the beginning of the year, your cheerleaders or Student Council can establish a theme that will encourage student support and further develop the tradition of good sportsmanship and positive school spirit. The theme should be displayed in the cafeteria, the front office, and in the gym (or at the stadium). Get other school and community groups involved, too.

Tryout Requirement

Some coaches require candidates at cheerleading tryouts to explain an idea that would boost positive behavior and promote good sportsmanship. This idea can be a written part of tryouts or part of an interview.

Administrative and Student Body Support

Meet with sport team coaches, administrators, student council representatives, faculty representatives, and your cheerleaders so that they can help select the activities that will enhance sportsmanship and school spirit at your school. Remember that everything you do will have an impact on the lives of young people.

Fundraising

Cheerleaders usually earn their own money for camps and supplies, and often must buy part or all of their uniforms. Since cheerleading is part of the athletic program, it should be part of the school budget plan for athletics. As the cheerleading coach, you will need to meet with your athletic director and other administrators to discuss how much funding is provided by the school. Be prepared for this meeting with a list of expenditures for your squad, including estimates for uniforms, supplies, camp, and equipment. The sad fact is that many cheerleading programs are not subsidized by their schools like the football or basketball programs are. Cheerleaders usually have to work long and hard to raise the money to buy uniforms, pompons, and megaphones. They either have to schedule fundraising activities or pay for their equipment, uniforms, and camp out of their own pocket.

Planning Issues

Establishing a fundraising plan in advance will help keep your program focused and organized. I suggest approving all fundraising activities right after tryouts so that cheerleaders, parents, faculty, and administrators know months in advance of any event. Fundraising activities can provide opportunities for communication, goal setting, leadership development, and self-confidence among your cheerleaders. In addition to the material presented in this chapter, an excellent book to help you with organizing fundraising events is William F. Stier's *Fundraising for Sport and Recreation*, published by Human Kinetics.

Here are nine key issues to remember when planning a fundraising event.

1. Establish a definite and worthwhile goal, challenging yet realistic. After you have met with administrators to find out what the school will pay for, meet with your cheerleaders to discuss the essentials that you must have. You may also want to schedule a meeting with the parents so they will understand why you are having fundraising events. Everyone needs to understand the goal and what the money will cover.

2. Define each individual's goals and make sure everyone is committed to success. Each person on the squad needs to take responsibility for their part in raising funds. I know of many schools that require an individual to make up the difference if they do not contribute equally to the squad goal.

3. Use publicity to enhance your success. Take advantage of as many media forms as possible such as posters at school and around your city, the school newspaper and public address system in the school, and radio announcements.

4. Keep accurate records. You may keep your own fundraising records, or you may ask a parent or one of the cheerleaders to keep everything organized for you. In some cases, one of the cheerleaders on the squad keeps all of the records. Make sure you stay well informed on the financial success of your fundraising program.

5. Make it a fun project. Your cheerleaders (and maybe their parents as well) should have direct input into the project you select. Everyone will probably work harder and support it more if they are having fun with the project. You can make it more fun by having a special party after the event, where beverages and snacks can be served. Or have someone film the event and watch the video at the party.

6. Charge a reasonable price. Before setting your price, you may want to check around and make sure that you are not charging too much or too little for your product or service. Ask for an outside opinion if you are unsure.

7. Set a firm end point. Your fundraising program should not drag on and on. A target stopping date should be established at the beginning.

8. Be enthusiastic at all times. You and your cheerleaders need to remember the importance of having a good attitude during your fundraising project, even if you should get discouraged halfway through. Remind yourselves of your goals, and plan a celebration when you meet them.

9. Remember to say thank you. People who support your program by participating in your fundraising events are very special and need to be appreciated. Besides saying

"thank you" with each sale, send notes of appreciation to individuals, clubs, organizations, or businesses who helped you in a significant way.

Ten Ways to Raise Money

There are many different ways to raise money for your cheerleaders. Some squads have traditional fundraising activities that they organize every year, such as a car wash, candy sale, or a community clinic; some squads like to try new ideas; and others use their fundraising activities to raise school spirit at the same time. The ideas presented here cover the spectrum of fundraising activities.

Jars

Have people put money in jars as a way of voting for something. A picture is taped on the outside of the jar for competitions such as Cutest Baby Picture, Guess the Baby, Sweetheart Day, or a Look-Alike Contest (students or teachers who look like movie stars, cartoon characters, or animals).

Books

Put together and print a book that will be sold, collecting the contents from teachers, students, and administrators: for instance, a recipe book, favorite motivational quotations, teen pages, or babysitting guide. You could also host a Book Fair.

"Grams"

Create variations of "telegrams" by delivering something to someone, usually personalized: for instance, a Cheer-O-Gram, Cookie Gram, Flower Gram, Candy Gram, Balloon-O-Gram, Candy Cane Gram for holidays, Heart-O-Gram for Valentine's Day, and Ghost Gram for Halloween.

Contests

Invent contests and charge an entry fee, or sometimes a voting fee: for instance, a Mr. America Pageant, Mr. and Ms. (School Name), Mr. and Ms. Spirit, or sponsor a road rally.

Raffles or Auctions

Solicit donated items for a raffle or auction: for instance, a gigantic stuffed mascot, giant spirit cake, computer, limousine ride, gift certificate, concert tickets, helium balloon ride, tanning sessions, movie tickets, one-of-a-kind quilt in your school colors, autographed equipment or uniforms from professional athletes.

Community Services

Exchange personal services for money: for instance, babysitting, window washing, party planning, organizing a community clean-up day (mow lawns, clean garages, wash windows, haul trash) or cheerleader day at McDonald's, a gas-o-rama (sell tickets in advance and pump gas at a local station), dog wash, car wash, garage sale, or airplane wash.

Food

Selling food is always a surefire way to make money if your school will allow it. Items that have been popular in many schools include candy bars, doughnuts or cinnamon rolls (before school), fruit, bags of penny candy, lollipops, pizza slices, and baked goods. Some schools donate the profits from a soft drink machine to the cheerleading program.

Spirit Items

There are some things you can sell that raise spirit while raising money. The school name and mascot can appear on these items: T-shirts, pennants, stadium cushions, minimegaphones, hats, bumper stickers, visors, mugs, towels, notebooks, key chains, pins, buttons, license plate frames, socks, student directories, stationery, plastic cups, minipompons, pillow cases, jackets, and stuffed animals.

Events

Organizing events such as these can raise money for your cheerleaders while entertaining people: present a video yearbook, dog show, dessert party, fashion show, talent show, powder puff football tournament, WPA (women pay all) Dance, hayride, school theme dance (such as Florida Fling), or offer continuing education classes or a Mom's Day Out babysitting service.

"Thons"

These are events that depend on pledges. People pledge so much money for how long each person can perform a certain feat: for instance, a Walk-A-Thon, Rock-A-Thon (rocking chair), Dance-A-Thon, Bounce-A-Thon, Talk-A-Thon, Bike-A-Thon, Eat-A-Thon, Jump-A-Thon, Ping-Pong-A-Thon, Crawl-A-Thon, Joke-A-Thon, Tricycle-A-Thon, Laugh-A-Thon, Nintendo-A-Thon, Roller Skate-A-Thon, Sing-A-Thon, Hula Hoop-A-Thon.

DIRTY CARS AND CLEAN FUN

Summer and car washes seem to go together. Almost every cheerleading squad in the country has a car wash to help earn money for uniforms or camp. We decided to have our car wash at a local McDonald's. The business was good for them and good for us at the same time (and they even advertised on their big sign). We printed and sold car wash tickets in advance, so that in case someone wasn't able to attend the actual car wash, we would at least have generated the revenue from a good intention.

Before the big event, we invited parents to help wash cars with us. We all brought buckets, soap, sponges, and kept a steady stream of cars rolling through. By the end of the car wash, there was not one dry T-shirt or one un-sunburned face. And asking the parents to help with the car wash made the day more fun for everyone.

Public Relations and Service

As school ambassadors and representatives, cheerleaders' involvement in community service and public relations can enhance the quality of your program and the quality of their experience. Good public relations is founded on two-way communication, effective organization, and positive visibility. You and your cheerleaders will be able to work smoothly with your administration, parents, sports programs, and the community if you strive for good public relations in every aspect of your program. Service projects provide opportunities for your cheerleaders to participate in the community as positive role models. They also provide opportunities for you to give something back to the community that supports your squad at games and fundraising events.

Community Activities

As you plan your public relations and service projects, keep in mind your philosophy and objectives as cheerleading coach. The projects you select should represent a deep commitment to helping young people grow through their involvement in the community. These projects are an important part of your program because they keep you and your cheerleaders connected to the community that you serve.

Letter to Parents

Send a letter to all parents at the beginning of the school year, listing the fall and winter sports and activities, special school projects, community service projects, fundraising programs, and plans for Homecoming. Invite the parents to become involved with the programs by asking them to return a Volunteer Form. (Chapter 2 contains additional ideas on communicating with parents.)

Elementary Spirit

Put on "spirit rallies" for local elementary school students. The spirit rally can also incorporate a "Say no to drugs" message.

Community Pride Video

Ask businesses and organizations for help in preparing a special community pride video that features interesting people, events, opportunities, and organizations in your community. Personally deliver one to the home of new people moving into your area. Include a special community reference guide and local phone book.

Cookie Thank You

At the end of the year, personally deliver a tin of cookies to each business that has supported your programs throughout the school year. The cookies can also be made for individuals who have contributed to the success of your program and the development of school spirit.

Spirit Gram

Print up special Spirit Grams and send thank you notes to individuals, businesses, and organizations (including parents and teachers) for their support during the school year.

Community Talent Night

Invite the community to try out for a community talent show that can be held in your auditorium or gymnasium. This event can help build community pride, and it can also be used as a fundraiser. Your cheerleaders will be able to showcase some of their cheers, chants, and dances too!

Continuing Education

Find qualified instructors to teach classes on topics of local interest, such as cake decorating, jewelry making, quilting, computers, health and fitness, or photography. These classes can be held at your school as a community service. Your cheerleaders can even conduct a class for elementary students, teaching basic cheer and dance techniques.

Parent Appreciation Rally

Invite parents to a special evening pep rally and show your appreciation by honoring special individuals or groups. You could present a "remember when" rally depicting school spirit traditions and dress from a generation ago and validate support for current programs with special awards or presentations.

Community Calendar

List all upcoming games, special events, programs, anniversaries, meetings, and community service projects. Distribute free or sell.

Appreciation Picnics

Set up periodic picnics during the year to show your appreciation to groups such as the administrators, the teachers, the band, the yearbook or newspaper staff, different clubs, and other special groups that contribute to the success and spirit of your school.

Traveling Talent Show or Spirit Rally

Put together a traveling talent show or spirit rally that performs for a children's hospital, a nursing home, or a veterans' hospital.

Adopt-A-Road

Adopt a portion of a local state roadway and keep it clean.

Booster Club Appreciation

Sponsor a Booster Club Appreciation Night where refreshments are served at a meeting, appreciation notes are distributed, and plans are announced for the members to be introduced at an upcoming game.

Read All About It

Ask your local newspaper if you can contribute a special community service column listing everything that is going on at school and all of the upcoming community service projects. This would be an excellent opportunity to announce your spirit events and to thank people for their support.

Health Fair

Have your cheerleaders organize a Health Fair at your school and offer vision exams, blood pressure tests, cholesterol tests, fingerprinting of children, home fire safety tips, and basic first aid procedures. Healthy snacks may also be distributed or sold. Your cheerleaders could also demonstrate basic stretches and an aerobic routine for fitness.

Discipline and Rules

Working within an established set of guidelines and regulations provides the cheerleaders with a framework for acceptable behavior. The rules, often appearing in a cheerleader constitution, build your program year after year because they set the standards and establish the expectations for the implementation of your program.

It is important to be consistent with the enforcement of the rules. As soon as the "best" cheerleader breaks a rule and does not receive the same penalty as the least skillful cheerleader, you will lose your credibility. A word of warning: Do not establish consequences or penalties that are unreasonable or so severe that you are not willing to enforce them with any member of the squad. The parents and the cheerleaders need to understand (even before tryouts) what is acceptable behavior. As you develop your own specific ideas, you may want to get input from the cheerleaders and their parents. Appendix A has an extensive list of items to help you develop your behavior guidelines. If you commit everything to writing and then welcome open discussion in case of challenges, you will eliminate most of the "gray areas" and provide high standards for your squad.

Summary

Here are the key points regarding the foundation upon which you may build your cheerleading program:

- The six tenets of your program are squad unity, leadership skills, sportsmanship and school spirit responsibilities, fundraising, public relations and service, and discipline and rules.
- Squad unity activities such as picnic practice, quote of the day, secret pal, hug circles, and a squad song build a bond of friendship and camaraderie that pervades the practices and performances.
- The eight leadership skill areas that can be enhanced through cheerleading activities are goal setting, organization, group process, problem solving and decision making, evaluation, communication, self-awareness, and uniting various clubs.
- Other ways to help build leadership on your squad include rotating captains and forming a spirit council.
- Consider uniting the clubs in your school to promote effective student leadership by holding monthly meetings of club presidents, starting a Club Hall of Fame, or making an all-school activities calendar.
- Build spirit and sportsmanship at your school through such things as a sportsmanship clinic, trophies and awards, setting a sportsmanship theme for the year, or conducting a clinic for elementary students.
- Set goals, be organized, and thoroughly plan each aspect of your fundraising projects.
- Ways of raising money for your cheerleading program include such ideas as a Cutest Baby Contest, a recipe book, a Cookie Gram, a Mr. or Ms. Spirit pageant, a raffle or auction, and food sales.
- To enhance community service and public relations, become involved in such things as making a community pride video, sending cookie thank yous, hosting a community talent night, setting up continuing education classes, and hosting an appreciation clinic or a health fair.
- As you develop your cheerleading program, be sure to give your cheerleaders a written list of their rules, regulations, guidelines, and expectations, or create a cheerleader constitution.

Part II
Coaching Plans

Chapter 5

Planning for the Season

As much as we may want to, we cannot escape filling out forms, scheduling events, and organizing related squad responsibilities. I have found that the more I can plan in advance, the calmer I feel about my upcoming season and the more fun I have. Advance planning will often determine the efficiency of your entire program, as well as keep your cheerleaders happy. I have heard many stories about coaches who waited until the last minute to order uniforms and, when they did not arrive in time for the first game, watched their squad cheer in T-shirts. Since my goal is to make coaching a positive experience for you, I hope this chapter will help you effectively plan for your season.

In your position as cheerleading coach, you are more than likely responsible for the entire cheerleading program, which spans the duration of your school's combined sports seasons. If you are coaching for a "season," you may need to have tryouts for the second half of the sports season as well and start your plan all over again. If you are a year-round coach, you can plan for the entire year. With foresight, patience, and follow-through, you can successfully pull everything together.

Following are eight areas I will discuss that will make your planning more manageable:

- Organizing your calendar of events
- Selecting your squad
- Planning for medical issues (physicals, injuries, emergencies)
- Working with assistants and incorporating supervision
- Scheduling practice times and facilities
- Preparing to cheer
- Managing squad travel
- Purchasing uniforms and supplies

Organizing Your Calendar of Events

Through the years, I have found that the more organized I am, the more I can accomplish. I have always used a calendar of events to keep me organized, and in turn I can help keep my cheerleaders organized. I write everything down on my calendar, which gives me a global view of the entire year as well as specific daily and weekly responsibilities.

Outline your entire year's events so you can plan your time wisely. What I like to do is to run off 8-1/2 by 11-inch monthly calendar sheets and type on them all practices, games, and special events: bus trips, pep rallies, fundraising events, competitions, and Homecoming activities. List times for each event and location. Other things that can be listed are birthdays, uniforms to wear, service projects, rotating captain, holiday events, and banquets. Be sure to announce changes at least two weeks in advance so that cheerleaders and their families can adjust their personal schedules.

Page 49 offers some suggestions, listed by season, for you to consider as you construct your calendar. Of course, each squad's calendar will be structured around the sports offered, game schedules, role in school spirit activities, traditions, and goals.

Selecting Your Squad

Cheerleading tryouts are a time of great excitement, preparation, and anxiety. The effectiveness of your cheerleading program is firmly rooted in your tryout procedures and organization. You establish your credibility, your program, and your expectations by how you conduct your tryouts. Even if your heart is pounding with apprehension and lack of confidence, you can organize very successful tryouts.

Most cheerleading tryouts occur in the spring so that squads can prepare over the summer and attend camp together. If tryouts are not held in the spring, you will need to conduct tryouts as soon as possible after school starts. Another option is to conduct a separate tryout after fall season sports for the upcoming winter season sports. If students from a different school or from middle school or junior high (going into high school) are allowed to try out for your squad, be sure to include them in all activities, which are generally held after school.

The tryout experience itself provides a terrific learning experience. Remember that the process and the plan is as important as the goal—selecting the best cheerleading squad to represent your school. You can help to "build people through cheerleading," even in the lives of those who don't make the squad. Every person who makes a commitment to your tryout procedure deserves the best from you. Always remember the heart, the feelings, and the self-esteem of each individual.

As a cheerleading coach, you face many choices when organizing your tryouts for the first time, or when evaluating a current procedure. As you read through the many suggestions, be sure to evaluate the ideas in relation to your personal philosophy, your program focus, your school, your sport programs, and your community culture. Remember to first get approval from your school administration for all your tryout procedures and policies before publicizing and holding the tryouts.

Pre-Tryout Preparation

Advance planning can make all the difference in the world. Pre-tryout preparation includes many tasks and, after you determine your plans, you will want to establish a timeline for completing them. First of all, obtain approval of your selected dates and times of your pre-tryout training sessions, as well as your exact tryout date. At the same time, schedule facilities for all of your sessions (pre-tryout and tryout). The area should be large enough to accommodate the sessions, with a high enough ceiling for stunts (if needed) and with mats (if needed). These sessions should be closed to spectators. After you have established your dates and location, publicize the tryouts with posters and school announcements.

Planning Your Tryouts

Take plenty of time to plan your tryouts because this important process forms the foundation for the rest of the season or the rest of the year. In order to build on this process from year to year, take notes on things that you want to remember for the next tryout session. Ask for feedback from administrators, judges, outgoing seniors, other coaches, and trusted

Seasonal Training Events

This sample list of calendar events is based on a spring tryout time and summer practices. Most coaches work with their cheerleaders sometime during the summer to help them prepare for summer camp and the upcoming football season.

SPRING

Physical examinations
Emergency plan
Injury management plan
Assistant coaches and supervision responsibilities
Pre-tryout training workshops
Tryouts
Season plan for skill development
Party for new squad
Assemble cheerleader notebooks
Elect captains
Schedule practice times and facilities for summer, fall, winter
Plan squad travel during sport seasons
Meet with parents
Choose, measure, and order uniforms
Fundraising for camp, supplies, etc.
Attend spring clinic
Decide on cheers and chants that will be used again this season
Start practices for camp
Work on decorations, spirit gifts, talent sharing for camp
Assign poster making
Set up standard practice schedule
Plan special summer event for squad unity

SUMMER

Set up summer practices
Creativity: plan cheers, chants, mounts, pyramids, etc.
Attend cheer camp
Select cheers, chants, mounts, pyramids, dances you will use from camp
Hold swim party
Set goals, objectives, and achievements
Hold end-of-summer rally at school
Hold clinic for local elementary students
Fundraising events
Make sure uniforms are ready
Keep up with ongoing conditioning program
Meet with fall sport coaches to discuss rules and sportsmanship
Get posters and banners made for the whole year
Squad picture taken
Set aside a three- to six-week span (moratorium) with no practices

FALL

Double-check on practices, facilities, and travel plans for season
Back-to-school pep rally
Homecoming
Set dates for football pep rallies
Include other fall sports
Make arrangements for out-of-town games
Divide responsibilities among squad members
Plan service project (such as Custodian Appreciation Day)
Plan spirit days
Parent days for fall sports
Serve as hosts for school events
Food baskets for needy at holidays
Special squad event for holidays
Fall clinic for area schools
Prepare for competition (rating or ranking)

WINTER

Organize for basketball and wrestling seasons
Change uniform in some way
Review cheers and chants
Fundraising event
Community service event
Special plans for tournaments
Review rules and regulations

confidantes. Your tryout procedure is a good way for you to communicate your coaching philosophy and establish your credibility.

There are many ways to organize your tryouts, and you will need to make some choices as to what specifically you want to do. I have made a checklist of important areas for you to consider in the light of your school's traditions and the type of squad you are developing. Ask yourself if each one is a component that you want for your tryouts.

___ Feeder school visits to explain and demonstrate program and distribute information packets
___ Pre-tryout training sessions (how many are needed for your particular tryout procedure?)
___ Mock tryout (complete run-through)
___ Candidate sign-up form
___ Candidate petition (to be signed by students and teachers)
___ Teacher evaluations
___ Skill sheet progression (minimum skills requirement)
___ Game rules test
___ Spirit planning component (for example, a poster or skit idea)
___ Essay (What I Can Do to Help Boost School Spirit, What Are the Essential Qualities of a Student Leader, How Does Cheerleading Help Me in the Future)
___ Video tryout for those who are unable to attend tryouts
___ Grade check
___ Conduct check
___ Private coaching for those who need more help

During Tryouts

Before conducting your tryouts, decide what you want on your judging form. Do you want your candidates to perform an individual cheer, a group cheer, a dance routine, or partner stunts? Do you want to include the school's fight song? What jumps are required or are all jumps optional? Look at the following checklist for items you may like to include on your judging form. Your requirements should reflect the type of squad you are developing (some squads do not dance, tumble, perform stunts, etc.).

___ Individual cheer (original or predetermined)
___ Group cheer (original or predetermined)
___ Individual chant (original or predetermined)
___ Group chant (original or predetermined)
___ Fight song (school's traditional fight song, new for tryouts, or original)
___ Dance routine (original or predetermined)
___ Jumps (list exact jumps and if there are optional jumps)
___ Tumbling pass (list gymnastic skills according to degree of difficulty)
___ Splits (only if your squad uses them)
___ Partner stunts (list predetermined stunts and if there are optional stunts)
___ Test of game rules
___ Personal interview (decide what the judges should look for)
___ Crowd involvement idea demonstrated

Judging

Cheerleading coaches typically choose their squad in one of two ways: They either assemble a panel of knowledgeable judges, or they select their squad independently. I recommend that you select your squad independently, the same as the football or basketball coaches would select their teams. If you are a new coach and do not feel comfortable selecting the squad on your own, then assemble a judging panel. This panel can be made up of any of the following: other cheer coaches in your area, college cheerleaders, professional cheer instructors, dance or gymnastics instructors, or your athletic director and sport team coaches if you feel they are knowledgeable about cheerleading.

Some cheerleading coaches also obtain input from teachers, typically by asking them to fill out an evaluation form for each candidate (see figure 5.1). You can use this confidential information to gain additional insight about the candidates trying out. Some coaches actually assign point values to the areas listed on the teacher evaluation form. Since I believe that cheerleaders are leaders who cheer, I favor the idea of having the teacher evaluations worth a certain percentage of the total (at least 25 percent). You will need to decide what you and your administrators feel is best for your program and your school.

Tryout Communication Packet

The purpose of a tryout communication packet is to totally outline your program,

Pre-Tryouts: Teacher Evaluation

Teacher ______________________________

Student ______________________________

The above student is trying out for a position on the cheerleading squad for next year. Please take a moment to evaluate him/her on these items.

Please score each item.

1. . .Poor 2. . .Below average 3. . .Average 4. . .Above average 5. . .Excellent

____ Attendance and punctuality

____ Honesty and dependability

____ Class conduct

____ Cooperative attitude

____ Ability to get along with others

____ Personality and enthusiasm

____ How well do you feel this person could represent this school as a member of the cheerleading squad?

Comments:

____

____

____

____ Approximate current grade

Teacher signature ______________________________

Class subject ______________________________

Figure 5.1 Teacher evaluation.

establish specific criteria for tryouts, and obtain parental permission. It's important for cheerleading candidates and their parents to clearly understand the responsibilities and procedures involved in cheerleading before tryouts. A commitment to your cheerleading program needs to be an informed commitment based on all of the facts. This tryout communication packet is distributed during the initial sign-up phase. Make announcements in advance as to where these can be picked up.

A sample Sign-Up and Parental Permission Form is shown in figure 5.2. Since there is always the possibility of injury during training sessions or tryouts themselves, have your cheerleaders' parents complete the Permission for Medical Treatment Form (figure 5.3) and the Insurance Status Form (figure 5.4) as well.

Your tryout communication packet should also state the eligibility requirements for trying out for cheerleader. State whether there is a minimum grade point average (usually a "C" average as on other teams), a multiple-sport participation policy (some schools do not allow cheerleaders to cheer at the same time they are playing on a sport team), a minimum course credit guideline, and the requirement of a medical examination form (as with all other teams). I have provided a sample Preparticipation Physical Evaluation

Sign-Up and Parental Permission Form

I have read the cheerleader constitution for *(name of school)* and I agree that I will at all times abide by those rules as long as I am a member of the *(name of school)* High School Cheerleading Squad. I promise to uphold the high standards of the squad in a way that will always be a credit to my school. I realize that failure to comply with these rules can mean my dismissal from the squad.

Candidate signature ______________________________ Date ________________

(Name of candidate) has signified a desire to become a cheerleader at *(name of school)*. If selected, there are certain responsibilities and obligations which must be assumed in order to remain a member of the squad. I have read the rules and regulations set forth in the cheerleading constitution. I will, insofar as I am able, see that these rules and regulations are carried out. I will, whenever questions arise, contact the cheerleader coach for clarification. I agree that my son/daughter will participate in all responsibilities as listed.

In case of emergency, Dr. ______________________ may be called at *(phone number)*. I hereby give *(candidate name)* permission to try out and take part in cheerleading activities at *(name of school)*.

Parent signature ______________________________ Date ________________

Phone numbers: Home ______________________ Work ______________________

Address ____

Figure 5.2 Sign-up and parental permission form.

Form (figure 5.5) in case your school or program does not have a health form for cheerleaders.

A copy of your rules and regulations (or cheerleader constitution) should be enclosed in the tryout communication packet, along with a sample judging form. Tryout procedures—pre-tryout and tryout schedules and locations, how tryouts will be conducted, and how the results will be posted—also need to be included. Two other items you may wish to enclose in your tryout packet are a calendar of your spring and summer practices and activities, plus a complete listing of all the safety rules your squad will be following.

Have the entire contents of your tryout communication packet approved by your principal or athletic director (or by both). This packet can establish a strong foundation for the rest of your season.

Pre-Tryout Training Sessions

These sessions are usually held in the gym and are closed to spectators. They should be organized and consistent with tryout procedures. Sessions should include a specific time for warm-up and stretching, instruction on required skills (cheers, chants, stunts, dances, jumps, tumbling), and practice time for individuals and groups. Allow time for questions and explanations. Be sure to end the sessions with a cooldown of light stretching or walking.

You should try to have from three to five required training sessions of one and a half to two hours in length. The training sessions can be conducted by you, outgoing seniors, former squad members, college cheerleaders, professional instructors, or qualified outside individuals. Make sure that your facilities are suitable for the sessions, and make arrangements for mats or sound equipment if needed.

Some coaches have a Skill Sheet listing expected progression of skills in order to try out. Qualified individuals are located at stations and rank candidates on such areas as jumps, stunts, and tumbling from beginning to advanced. Each candidate must "pass" a

Permission for Medical Treatment Form

In the event of an emergency occurring while my son/daughter is on a school-sponsored practice, performance, or trip, I hereby grant permission to the school and to its employees to take whatever action deemed necessary. In the event that I cannot be reached, I hereby authorize the school and/or its employees to give consent for my son/daughter,

____ to receive medical treatment.

Home phone ____________________ Business phone ____________________

Address ____

Person to be notified other than parent or guardian in emergency:

Emergency person ____________________ Phone ____________________

Family doctor ____________________ Phone ____________________

If you do not give permission or authorization for consent to medical treatment, what procedure should be followed? (Please state)

____

____

Insurance information ____

Date ______________ ______________________________
Parent/Guardian signature

Figure 5.3 Permission for medical treatment form.

Insurance Status Form

Please check one:

____ I will take out (or have already taken out) the athletic insurance policy offered through the school.

____ My son/daughter is fully covered by insurance carried by his/her parent(s) and the school will not be liable for any injury that occurs during cheerleading practice, contests, or travel to and from cheerleading activities.

Name of insurance company ____

Date ______________ ______________________________
Parent/Guardian signature

Figure 5.4 Insurance status form.

Preparticipation Physical Evaluation Form

Physical Examination Date ____________

Name ______________________________ Age _______ Date of birth ______________

Complete	Limited	Height _______ Weight _______ Blood pressure _____/_____ Pulse _______						
		Vision R 20/ _______ L 20/ _______ Corrected: Y N Pupils _______						
			Normal	Abnormal findings				Initials
		Cardiopulmonary						
		Pulses						
		Heart						
		Lungs						
		Tanner stage	1	2	3	4	5	
		Skin						
		Abdominal						
		Genitalia						
		Musculoskeletal						
		Neck						
		Shoulder						
		Elbow						
		Wrist						
		Hand						
		Back						
		Knee						
		Ankle						
		Foot						
		Other						

Clearance:

A. Cleared

B. Cleared after completing evaluation/rehabilitation for ______________________

C. Not cleared for: ☐ Collision

☐ Contact

☐ Noncontact ___Strenuous ___Moderately strenuous ___Nonstrenuous

Due to ____

Recommendation: ____

____

____

Name of physician ______________________ Date ______________

Address ______________________ Phone ______________

Signature of physician ______________________

Figure 5.5 Athletic preparticipation physical evaluation form.

minimum skills requirement in order to try out.

Here are some suggestions for Skill Sheet progressions. The items listed go from beginning to intermediate to advanced.

- Jumps: spread jump ____
  herkie jump ____
  toe touch ____
- Stunts: back thigh stand ____
  shoulder sit ____
  shoulder stand ____
- Tumbling: forward roll ____
  cartwheel ____
  round-off ____
  front handspring ____
  round-off back handspring ____

Pre-Tryout Meeting With Candidates and Parents

I recommend that you have a meeting with the candidates and their parents before tryouts to go through the information in the tryout communication packet. The purpose of this meeting is to make sure that everyone fully understands the policies, responsibilities, and commitment involved in the cheerleading program. This meeting will provide an excellent opportunity for candidates and parents to ask questions and clarify any part of the tryout procedure or any aspect of your program.

At the beginning of the meeting, when you introduce yourself to the group, describe your experience and philosophy and give out your phone number along with good times to contact you. Introduce your athletic director and principal if possible (determine in advance if they will address the group) and your assistant coach(es). Go through all of the forms (parental permission, insurance, permission for treatment, etc.). Remind everyone of the required health examination that needs to be on file with the school before tryouts.

After you have explained the tryout procedures, ask for questions. Some parents may want to discuss time commitment, transportation, fundraising, or possible out-of-pocket expenses. By the end of this meeting the candidates and their parents should have a clear picture of your program and of tryouts themselves. You are now ready for the actual tryout session.

Tryout Session

Even if you have decided to select the squad yourself, you still may want input from additional judges. You can take the information from their judging forms and their comments into consideration as you make your final selection. Throughout this section, I will refer to "the judges," meaning you and your helpers, whether their points actually count or not in determining the final scores.

The candidates are usually very nervous for tryouts, so I recommend that they try out individually and in small groups in front of the judges with no other spectators. Before tryouts begin, make sure that the candidates stretch thoroughly (usually graduating seniors lead this session). Have candidates draw numbers for the order or assign numbers according to an alphabetical listing. Attach numbers to the front or back of T-shirts by using a self-adhesive label, or use small safety pins for a number written on felt or fabric. Since there could be significant time lapses between when candidates with lower early numbers and those with higher numbers try out, make sure that the candidates trying out later in the session stretch again before they go in front of the judges.

Once the tryouts begin, I find the best way to record my impressions is to use a Judging Form. The judging form should reflect the skill areas that are to be represented on your squad during the season. For instance, if jumps are extremely important on your squad, the Judging Form will reflect this by how many jumps are to be performed and how many points they are worth in reference to the total points. Many tryouts include both an individual cheer and a group cheer, and some will have a dance segment. A sample Judging Form is presented in figure 5.6.

Try to keep the tryout running smoothly and efficiently, for both the judges' and the candidates' sakes. If someone makes a major mistake and asks to start again, I think you should let them. However, I would not allow candidates to do everything again because they think they can do a better job the second time around. Remember to smile and be supportive of each candidate.

PULLED MUSCLES

At one point, trying out for the cheerleading squad was the most important thing in my life. I was attending a brand new high school

Tryouts: Judging Form

Physical Appearance (10 points possible)

____ Neat, clean, physically fit, good posture, moderate make-up, hair tied back

Individual Cheer (5 points each)

____ Execution
____ Motions/sharpness
____ Voice/timing
____ Jump(s)
____ Degree of difficulty
____ Pep/enthusiasm
____ Facial expression
____ Overall quality

Group Cheer (5 points each)

____ Execution
____ Motions/sharpness
____ Voice/timing
____ Facial expression
____ Pep/enthusiasm
____ Overall quality

Jumps (5 points each)

____ Herkie
____ Toe touch
____ Hurdler
____ Optional jump

Gymnastics (points vary)

____ Splits (2 points)
____ Cartwheel (2 points)
____ Round-off (3 points)
____ Round-off/back handspring (5 points)
____ Optional gymnastics maneuver I (5 points)
____ Optional gymnastics maneuver II (5 points)

Dance Routine (5 points each)

____ Execution
____ Rhythm/timing
____ Showmanship/confidence
____ Pep/enthusiasm
____ Facial expression
____ Overall quality

Figure 5.6 Judging form.

and trying out for the freshman squad. Since cheerleading was not offered in lower grades, this was my first attempt to make a squad. I could not talk or think of anything else. I visualized myself being a cheerleader and having the most fun of my entire life. The day of tryouts was the longest day in history, but I finally made it to the gym at the end of the day to change clothes and prepare for the actual tryout session. We had all drawn numbers for the order of performance. During each person's tryout time, the rest of us were supposed to be stretching over to the side in preparation for our time in front of the judges.

Right in the middle of someone's performance, a loud pop erupted in the room: It was the sound of my hamstring ripping as I attempted the splits without stretching first. The damage was such that I was not able to try out. Since our school only had freshman and senior cheerleaders, I knew I had a three-year wait before my name could appear on a judge's sheet. As I look back on that most disappointing day, I don't know which muscle hurt the most—my hamstring or my heart.

Announcing the Squad

Following are some suggestions for announcing who made the squad. Select the method that best represents the philosophy of your program.

- Announce the names to the entire group after tryouts.
- Post names or numbers of squad members selected.
- Phone, send a letter, or meet personally with individuals.
- Leave names on an answering machine or school recording.
- Announce names on a local radio station at a prearranged time.
- Have outgoing seniors contact new squad members individually.

Sometimes, how you announce the squad will have a dramatic affect on those candidates that do not make the squad. If the names are announced to the entire group, the candidates that did not make the squad may have a difficult time handling their disappointment (which can be hard on you as well). Be prepared for varying reactions. Many coaches elect to post the names or numbers, either because tallying the judging ballots takes a long time and the results are not available until a few hours after tryouts, or because they have found that candidates would feel more comfortable dealing with the results privately. I recommend that you announce your squad to the entire group as soon after tryouts as possible. If there is a time delay, then I think that the results should be posted.

Planning for Medical Issues

The three most important medical issues are physical examinations, acute injuries, and emergencies. You need to be well-prepared to handle these concerns.

Physical Examinations

Physicals are required for all athletes. The medical screening form or physical form may differ from state to state, district to district, city to city. The important thing to remember is that you *must* require a physical examination form from each cheerleader. Make sure that you study each physical or health form so that you can be alerted to potential problem areas such as asthma, heart conditions, or previous injuries. It is imperative that you have knowledge of each cheerleader's medical history. If there is any part of a cheerleader's medical history that they request be kept confidential, be sure to honor that request.

If you do not have access to a physical form, I recommend the Preparticipation Physical Evaluation Form illustrated in figure 5.5.

Along with medical screening, you should have proof of the participant's insurance. You may want to use the sample shown in figure 5.4 or a form provided by your school.

INFORMATION WITHHELD

I was attending a cheerleading camp where I lived in the dorm with the cheerleaders. Early one morning, some cheerleaders frantically pounded on my door and asked me to come quickly. A cheerleader had fallen in the shower and appeared to be in the middle of a seizure. I raced down the hallway and into the shower. We pulled the girl from the shower and called for emergency personnel immediately. We were scared for her, but she was lucky and did not experience any injury or complications from the seizure or the fall. The girl's coach was not living in the dorm with us, but I saw her later that day. She was totally surprised that one of her cheerleaders had experienced an epileptic seizure and said, "This information was not submitted on her physical form. I wish I would have known." As I walked away from her, I realized again the importance of having all important health conditions listed on the physical form. Information that is withheld can be potentially dangerous.

Acute Injuries

Some cheerleading squads are served by the trainer for the athletic team or a local sports physical therapist in case of injury. Make arrangements in advance for your cheerleaders to receive informed attention and service in case of injury during practice, games, or competition.

Since ankle injuries are the most common mishap for cheerleaders, you should have ice, plastic bags, and elastic wraps available at each practice and game. If you do not know how to wrap an ankle, make arrangements to learn from a sport coach, athletic trainer, or physical therapist. Proper management of soft tissue (ligaments, tendons, muscle) injuries when they occur can help diminish the amount of time a cheerleader is out of action.

WHEN IN DOUBT, CHECK IT OUT

When a cheerleader sprained her ankle during practice, I quickly wrapped the ankle, elevated it, and kept ice on it, alternating every 20-30 minutes with ice on, ice off. This quick action brought her back to full activity much faster than if I had done nothing. If her ankle had continued to cause pain and problems, I would have recommended that her family take her to see a doctor. I believe that "if in doubt, check it out."

Emergencies

There may come a time when you will be faced with an emergency situation. You will be more prepared to handle an emergency (such as a fall or seizure) if you do the following in advance.

- Always have a copy of every cheerleader's health card or physical form, plus a signed consent for medical treatment and insurance information.
- Always have change available for phone calls.
- If you do not have the 911 emergency service in your area, always have the local emergency numbers available.
- Discuss emergency procedures with your cheerleaders in advance. Squad members should remain calm at all times.

It is extremely important to have authorization from the parent or guardian for the coach to take whatever action is deemed necessary in an emergency. See figure 5.3 for a sample permission form you could use.

When a severe injury occurs (for example, a head, neck, or back injury or severe fracture) do not move the victim unless he or she is in a life-threatening situation. Know how to activate the emergency medical system at all times. I strongly recommend CPR and first aid classes for all cheerleading coaches (refer to courses offered by ASEP in your area).

Because you are responsible for the health, safety, and well-being of your cheerleaders, and because cheerleaders do get injured, consider obtaining an insurance policy that will protect you in case of a lawsuit. I have been asked to give a deposition on a lawsuit that was filed against a cheerleading coach over an injury that occurred during tryouts. Make sure you find out how you are covered in case of a lawsuit, and compare it to how the sport team coaches are covered. In addition to a policy your school might provide, I recommend that you join the National Federation Interscholastic Spirit Association. For a low annual fee, you receive $1,000,000 in personal liability insurance, along with other benefits and privileges.

Assistant Coaches and Supervision

Some cheerleading coaches are lucky enough to have an assistant coach. The majority of cheerleading coaches have an assistant coach only in their dreams. If you are one of the lucky ones, make sure your assistant has a thorough understanding of the responsibilities, goals, and philosophy of your program. Your assistant should work closely with you during the year and perhaps specialize in some aspect of the program in order to ease your coaching burdens. Some assistant coaches specialize in handling skill development, conditioning, and strength building, and some take over all of the paperwork and behind-the-scenes responsibilities.

If your squad needs additional assistance, such as for a special performance or competition, you may want to hire a private coach with special expertise areas. The private coach could be a college or university cheerleader, a professional instructor who works for a camp company, or a gymnastics or dance instructor. But before hiring a private coach, be sure to check with your state high school association to verify if a private coach is allowed. A private coach can help your squad master new skills in a weak area, provide a good source of creative ideas, and also help improve the overall effectiveness of the squad's cheering skills.

Your assistant coach can also help you with one of your primary responsibilities—supervision! Your cheerleaders should not be allowed to practice or cheer at a game unless you or your assistant are with them. Because safety may not always be on their minds, your cheerleaders need your constant vigilance at every practice and game. They must know that you are serious about safety. You can convince them of that by discussing the safety rules at every practice. I made signs with pictures and explanations of the safety rules so that we would always have them on hand.

You and your assistant should have an organized plan for each practice and game, and make sure your cheerleaders know that goofing around is not tolerated. I use posterboard to list everything that needs to be accomplished at a specific practice or event. The size of the posterboard makes it easy for everyone to read and follow the plan. I refer to it often and make it available for everyone to see.

Even when I am not talking with my cheerleaders, my presence at every event serves as a nonverbal, constant reminder that I care about them as people, that I care about the process of my program, and that I care about their safety.

Scheduling

Cheerleaders rarely have their own facilities, and their practice times usually must rotate around when teams are not practicing in the main gym(s). Quite often, cheerleaders are left with inadequate practice facilities. The practice area should have a suitable surface (not concrete or tile-over-concrete), have mats available, be well-lit, be free of obstructions, and be located away from excessive noise or distractions. Your cheerleaders should not practice in the school hallways! I suggest that you meet with the sport team coaches and athletic director to schedule your practice times in a gym.

Typical practice times for cheerleaders are before or after school, a weekday evening, Saturday mornings, or Sunday evenings. Some squads utilize a combination of the above, but most practice right after school. Some schools schedule a class period every day for cheerleaders to practice and plan spirit activities (and may also give a physical education credit for this class). Many of the practices during the summer months are held outside the school in the early morning hours.

Preparing to Cheer

How do cheerleaders come up with the cheers and chants that they use to support the team and lead the crowd? They use cheers and chants from the year(s) before, make up new ones, and learn many from camp. Make sure you help your cheerleaders make their selections of traditional favorites based on crowd response and appropriateness. Do not let your cheerleaders lead cheers or chants that are negative, show poor sportsmanship, or use cuss words or words that are suggestive.

One way to add new material to a repertoire is to divide the squad into creativity groups and have them try different ideas to help get started on creating new cheers and chants. One idea is to write out the words to current or collected cheers and chants, cut the lines apart, and have the groups randomly select different lines to form into new cheers and chants. Another possibility is to give each group a theme such as a mascot cheer, school color cheer, score chant, or defense chant. After your cheerleaders make up the new cheers and chants, they perform them in front of the whole group. One more way to encourage creativity is to write out on three-by-five-inch individual cards all of the basic words that are used in cheers and chants: for instance, Go, Fight, Win, Score, Victory, Defense, your mascot name, or your school colors. Each group draws two or three words and builds a chant. The results can be very creative.

During practices, when your cheerleaders are making final selections for their cheers and chants, they may want to write the words on posterboard and use these as cue cards. As they cheer, they merely glance down at the posterboard if in doubt about what chant or cheer to do next. Some squads print the words to cheers and chants on paper and tape the sheet inside their megaphones. If the captain or head cheerleader is not responsible for starting all cheers and chants, the squad members may each take responsibility for a specific number of cheers and chants to remember and to start during the game (depending on the game situation). By the time your squad cheers for their first game, they should have all of their cheers and chants thoroughly ready.

Managing Squad Travel

Some schools provide bus transportation for away games, and some do not. Find out whether your school has a policy of mandatory bus transportation. Some cheerleaders ride the team bus, some ride with parents, some drive themselves, and some do not attend away games (unless they are conference games). I recommend that cheerleaders do not drive themselves to away games. The school should provide transportation for your squad. As the coach, you should not be driving the cheerleaders in your personal vehicle.

If you are responsible for scheduling a bus for away events, be sure to fill out and send in the appropriate forms in advance. Some schools schedule a "spirit bus" that carries cheerleaders, parents, and students to away games. If your school requires a special form for bus riders to fill out in advance, make sure you take care of these details efficiently. Remember that there must be a chaperon on the bus with the cheerleaders—either you, an assistant, or a parent.

Purchasing Uniforms and Supplies

Right after tryouts, assemble the measurements of your squad members so you can begin to order uniforms. Since uniforms are often tailor-made, allow plenty of time for manufacture and delivery. Many squads "pass down" uniforms and then merely add something new each year.

Uniform choices can include different combinations of a sweater or sweatshirt, skirt, vest or top, pants or shorts. A lot of squads will plan a mix 'n match set of choices for different seasons. For instance, a vest or top can be worn alone or with a turtleneck top underneath. Pants can be worn with a sweater for football, and a skirt can be worn with a vest for basketball. The uniform choice usually depends on the weather, the facilities (inside or out), and the sport. Include your squad members in decisions about uniforms if possible.

There are many professional cheerleading uniform companies across the country. Some of these companies have representatives that will come to your school to measure your cheerleaders, show you uniform samples, and help you fill out the order form. If you do not already receive catalogs from uniform companies, refer to the list of uniform companies in Appendix B.

When you are making selections for your uniforms, take plenty of time to select your shoes. The quality, support, and construction of the shoes can make the difference between a sprained ankle and safety-conscious cheering. If you are unsure about making the shoe decision, talk with representatives from uniform companies or talk to a sports physical therapist to find out what shoes your squad should be wearing for maximum support and comfort. For instance, a squad that performs partner stunts and pyramids might select a shoe that is different from a squad that never performs partner stunts and pyramids. Cheerleaders should never wear canvas shoes that offer no support!

The basic supplies and props used by cheerleaders are megaphones and pompons. The megaphones are used to lead the crowd and can be decorated with vinyl tape striping or a painted mascot. Pompons accentuate the words to cheers and chants, and are also used when performing the school fight song or a dance routine.

Cheerleaders also use crowd involvement signs, which should be made in advance and used during practices. Crowd involvement signs usually have words that are repeated during a cheer such as GO, FIGHT, WIN, the mascot name, or a phrase like GO BIG RED. These signs can be used during games and pep rallies to unify the crowd. They are usually posterboard-size (two-by-three feet) with dark easy-to-read letters. If you or your squad members are not able to letter neatly with markers, use large (12-inch) stencils to trace, and then color in. The signs can also be laminated or made into various shapes (such as a box or three-sided pyramid with different words on each side). Chapter 9 provides further suggestions on how to use crowd involvement ideas.

Summary

Whether planning for a season or a year, remember these important suggestions:

- Make a calendar of events, listing practices, games, special events, and other items important to the effectiveness of your program.
- Pre-tryout preparations should include scheduling facilities, printing and distributing a tryout communication packet, and meeting with your candidates and their parents.
- Prepare your candidates for tryouts both mentally and physically with pre-tryout training sessions.
- Make sure you have a complete up-to-date physical form and proof of insurance for each cheerleader.
- Be informed about your emergency medical system at all times.
- Consider training an assistant coach to make your job more manageable.
- Hire a private coach if needed (and if allowed in your state) for skill development and special event choreography.
- Supervise all practices, games, and performances yourself.
- Meet with sport team coaches and the athletic director to schedule facilities and practice times.
- Sponsor creativity sessions during practice to generate more cheers and chants to add to your repertoire.
- Make detailed arrangements for bus trips in advance, and be sure to fill out the proper forms for requests.
- Order uniforms and supplies soon after the squad is selected.

Chapter 6

Courtesy of Mahomet-Seymour High School

Preparing for Practices

Cheerleaders are athletes who cheer for other athletes. But since most cheerleaders serve their school year-round, spanning numerous sports seasons, their physical demands are different from other athletes'. In this chapter I will give suggestions on how to plan for and conduct effective practice sessions, including information on stretching, conditioning, strengthening, and skill development. Your practice, in essence, is your program-in-motion. As you develop athletic abilities in your cheerleaders, you also raise their confidence, their performance level, and their commitment to your squad. A successful practice provides a solid foundation for a successful program. Since you work so closely with your cheerleaders during these practice sessions, I will also address body image issues: healthy habits and eating disorders.

Conducting Practices

Regularly scheduled and required practice sessions are crucial to building the skills necessary to meet the physical demands of cheerleading. As the coach, you should have a specific plan for each practice, making adjustments when needed. If you have an organized plan for practice, you will be able to allot time for each phase of development.

As your cheerleaders learn what is expected of them by how you structure your practice, you will be able to get more accomplished and your job may become a little easier.

Why should cheerleaders stretch, condition, strengthen, and develop their physical skills? Here are some of the benefits you will discover as you prepare for and conduct your practices:

- Confidence, pride, and positive self-image
- Injury prevention
- Flexibility and agility
- Muscle strength and endurance
- Cardiovascular conditioning
- Reduced body fat
- Overall health
- High level of performance

Arrival and Preparation

Allow time for your cheerleaders to go to the restroom, change into practice clothes and athletic shoes, remove jewelry, tie hair back, and socialize briefly. The mats should be pulled out, the practice area should be clear and free from distractions, and the music should be tested (if dances will be practiced or if music is used for stretching). Before starting the physical practice, you can make announcements, discuss the goals for the practice, and comment on the success or achievements of the previous athletic event. This pre-practice time will help your cheerleaders physically and mentally shift gears, and prepare them to focus on the goals of the practice.

General Body Warm-Up

A good way to get the blood to the muscles is to have your cheerleaders jog one or two easy laps around the gym or track before you begin your stretching session. If you would prefer, your general body warm-up can be a short, invigorating dance routine to music, such as your fight song or a favorite set of eight-counts. Sending the blood to the muscles before stretching will enable your cheerleaders to get a better stretch and will help prevent injuries while stretching.

Stretching Program

Your cheerleaders should do their stretching exercises as a group to keep everyone focused on the task at hand and so that you can observe the quality of each person's involvement. This session should last at least 15 minutes (the exact length of time will vary with the content of the practice; a longer stretching session will be required if the emphasis is placed on tumbling). The stretching program should be organized, consistent, and thorough. All major muscle groups should be included in the stretch, such as neck, arms, shoulders, back, trunk, hamstrings, groin, hips, quads, abdominals, calves, and ankles. Remember these basics for any stretching routine:

- Relaxed, sustained stretches should be held 10-20 seconds (to increase flexibility, hold for 20-30 seconds).
- Never bounce a muscle.
- Know your limits. A small amount of discomfort may be expected. Do not overstretch. If you feel mild tension, then relax.
- Relax the neck when bent over and never jerk the neck to any position.

STRETCHING KNOWLEDGE

I guess you just never know when something that you have learned will transfer to something totally unrelated. I had been working with cheerleaders about ten years before my son Ray was born. After he was diagnosed with cerebral palsy, my husband (who had been a college cheerleader) and I enrolled him in an early intervention program when he was six months old. I remember his first physical therapy session at the Infant Development Center. The therapist started showing us the stretching exercises that we were to perform on Ray's spastic leg muscles. We looked at each other and smiled. "We know how to do these. We are cheerleaders."

Following are some examples of basic stretches to include in your warm-up routine. If you'd like more information about types of stretches and proper stretching techniques, contact Human Kinetics for Michael J. Alter's *Sport Stretch* book.

BASIC INDIVIDUAL STRETCHES

Name: **Neck Stretch** (see figure 6.1a)

Starting Position: Standing, legs shoulder-width apart.

Steps:
1. Tuck chin into chest, hold for 10-20 seconds.
2. Lift chin up, head back, hold for 10-20 seconds.
3. Face forward, put left ear to left shoulder, hold for 10-20 seconds.
4. Return forward, repeat on the right side, hold for 10-20 seconds.
5. Return forward, look to left (behind), hold for 10-20 seconds.
6. Return forward, look to right (behind), hold for 10-20 seconds.

Figure 6.1a

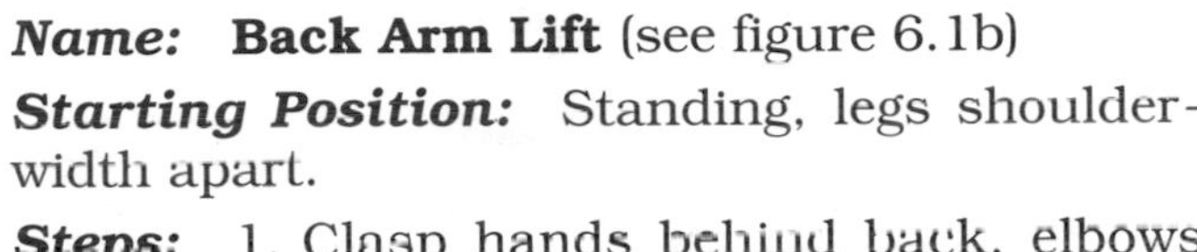

Name: **Back Arm Lift** (see figure 6.1b)

Starting Position: Standing, legs shoulder-width apart.

Steps:
1. Clasp hands behind back, elbows straight.
2. Lift arms up (still clasped) and lean head back.
3. Bend over at the waist, lifting arms up and leaning head back at the same time, hold for 10-20 seconds.
4. Slowly return to starting position and then repeat.

Figure 6.1b

Name: **Side Leans** (see figure 6.1c)

Starting Position: Standing, legs shoulder-width apart.

Steps:
1. Clasp hands over head, elbows straight.
2. Lean to left, hold 10-20 seconds.
3. Return to starting position, then lean to right, hold 10-20 seconds.
4. Repeat left lean, then right lean.

Figure 6.1c

BASIC INDIVIDUAL STRETCHES *(continued)*

Name: **Calf Muscle Stretch** (see figure 6.1d)

Starting Position: Place hands shoulder height on a wall. Place feet in forward stride position (one in front of the other), keeping back heel on the floor.

Steps:
1. Place weight on forward (bent) leg and slowly lean forward, hold 10-20 seconds.
2. Change positions, moving opposite leg forward, and repeat.

Figure 6.1d

Name: **Ankle Roll** (see figure 6.1e)

Starting Position: Standing, legs shoulder-width apart.

Steps:
1. Slowly roll ankle outward and inward three times.
2. Repeat with other ankle.

Figure 6.1e

Name: **Hamstring Stretch** (see figure 6.1f)

Starting Position: Seated, with legs straight out in front of you.

Steps:
1. Reach arms forward over legs (grasp ankles with hands if possible) and lean forward, hold 10-20 seconds.
2. In same position, point toes forward, hold 10-20 seconds.
3. In same position, point toes straight up, hold 10-20 seconds.

Figure 6.1f

BASIC INDIVIDUAL STRETCHES *(continued)*

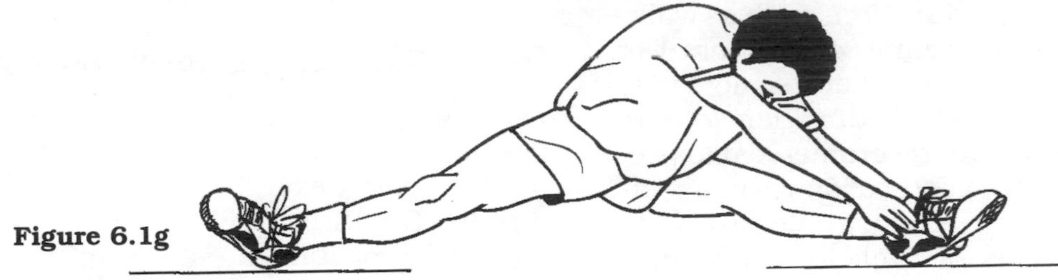

Figure 6.1g

Name: **Straddle Stretch** (see figure 6.1g)

Starting Position: Seated, with legs out in straddle position (knees facing up and legs flat on floor in at least a 90-degree angle to each other).

Steps:
1. Lean over left leg, point toes forward, hold 10-20 second.
2. Lean over right leg, point toes forward, hold 10-20 seconds.
3. Lean over left leg, point toes straight up, hold 10-20 seconds.
4. Lean over right leg, point toes straight up, hold 10-20 seconds.

Name: **Groin Stretch** (see figure 6.1h)

Starting Position: Seated, bend knees and bring feet toward you. Hold soles of feet together.

Steps:
1. Sit straight, slowly push knees to ground, hold 10-20 seconds.
2. Relax and repeat.

Figure 6.1h

The important thing to remember when planning your stretching session is that everyone stretches all muscle groups before any type of practice or cheering activities. Sometimes your cheerleaders can give suggestions for stretches to use at practices based on previous training in sports, gymnastics, or dance. Be sure to screen these suggestions in private to make sure they are not harmful. There are many other possible stretching exercises you can use, such as some that the football, basketball, gymnastics, or wrestling coaches might use. I would also suggest that you evaluate stretches that you may learn at camp, from other cheerleading coaches, or from books and magazines about cheerleading (see Cheerleading Resources in Appendix B).

Incorporating ideas from various sources will give you more choices, provide variety, and keep practices more interesting. If you decide to standardize your stretching program (and this is a good idea, too) always make sure your cheerleaders do not rush through them. Your cheerleaders need to maintain a serious attitude about the stretching time at each practice.

Conditioning Program

The body has two basic energy systems, anaerobic and aerobic. Activities of short duration (two to three minutes) primarily use the anaerobic system, which uses energy sources that are immediately available to the muscles. An example of a training activity for anaerobic energy is "hollow sprints," which consist of 60 yards of sprinting, 60 yards of jogging, and 60 yards of walking. Repeat sequence until fatigued. Another example would be jumping rope for a short period of time at high intensity. When cheerleaders are performing their cheers, chants, dances, and stunts, they are utilizing their anaerobic system.

Activities of longer duration, such as walking, jogging, and bicycling, can be used to improve aerobic capacity. Aerobic activities lasting 20-30 minutes in duration four to five times per week are recommended to promote and maintain good cardiovascular fitness. Cheerleaders need aerobic fitness to meet the demands of a cheerleading program.

Your practices should have both aerobic and anaerobic activities to help you strive for peak performance in your athletes. As you and your squad set performance goals for the year, you may want to request individual commitment to additional aerobic and anaerobic conditioning outside of the established conditioning during normal practices.

Strengthening Exercises

Depending on what kind of program you are coaching, you will need to implement strengthening exercises for specific muscle groups. The three I will discuss are exercises for developing jump strength, ankle strength, and wrist strength.

Jumps: Special Strengthening

Strengthening your legs, abdomen, and arms will be the key to improved jumps. A few of the most effective strengthening exercises are push-ups, tuck jumps, toe raises, and V-lifts.

Figure 6.2a

Name: **Push-Up** (see figure 6.2a)

Starting Position: Body parallel to floor, back level, toes on floor, arms locked with hands shoulder-width apart.

Steps:
1. Keep body tight and straight.
2. Lower yourself to the ground.
3. Push back up. Repeat as many times as possible.

Name: **Tuck Jump** (see figure 6.2b)

Starting Position: Standing, legs are slightly apart.

Steps:
1. Jump up, bringing knees as high as possible in front of body.
2. Slap your shins when you are airborne.
3. Bring arms out to a "T" position as you land.
4. Repeat as many times as possible.

Figure 6.2b

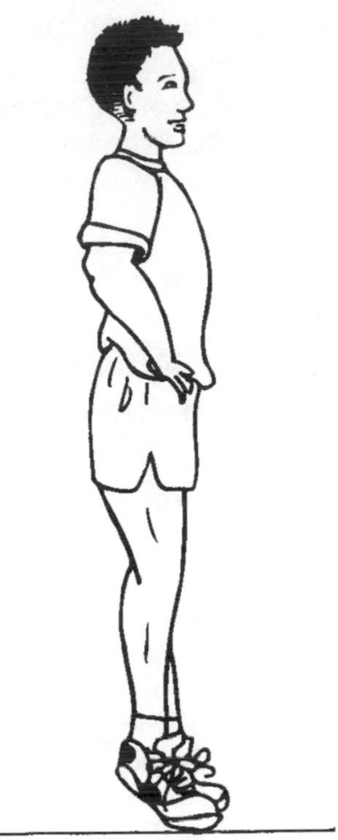

Figure 6.2c

Name: **Toe Raise** (see figure 6.2c)

Starting Position: Standing, feet are slightly apart.

Steps:
1. Raise up on toes to flex calf muscles, hold for 10-20 seconds.
2. Lower down to flat feet and knees slightly bent.
3. Repeat as many times as possible.

Name: **V-Lift** (see figure 6.2d)

Starting Position: Lying down on back, hands in front of chest or behind head, legs straight.

Steps:
1. Raise legs two inches off floor in a straddle position (legs at 90 degrees) with toes pointed.
2. Lift upper body halfway while lifting legs, hold for 10-20 sec.
3. Try to fold in half.
4. Lower, but do not allow head or feet to touch the floor.
5. Repeat as many times as possible.

Figure 6.2d

Ankle Strengthening

Ankle strengthening is often overlooked but is very important to your cheerleading program. Ankle injuries are the number one cause of discomfort and loss of participation time. The three exercises I recommend are the leg extension exercise, the toe raise exercise presented previously (see figure 6.2c), and heel walking.

Name: **Leg Extension** (see figure 6.3a)

Starting Position: Seated, making sure knees are flexed to a 90-degree angle.

Equipment Needed: #107 large rubber band (available in office supply stores)

Steps:

1. Place rubber band around both feet at the base of toes.
2. While one foot remains stationary, pull the rubber band outward and upward with the other foot, keeping heel in place, hold for 5-10 seconds.
3. Return to starting position as slowly as possible.
4. Repeat for 10-20 minutes once or twice a day.

Figure 6.3a

Name: **Heel Walking** (see figure 6.3b)

Starting Position: Standing, legs are slightly apart.

Steps:

1. Raise toes, standing on heels, hold for 5-10 seconds.
2. Maintain position walking gently in place for 10-20 seconds.
3. Lower slowly.
4. Repeat for two minutes.

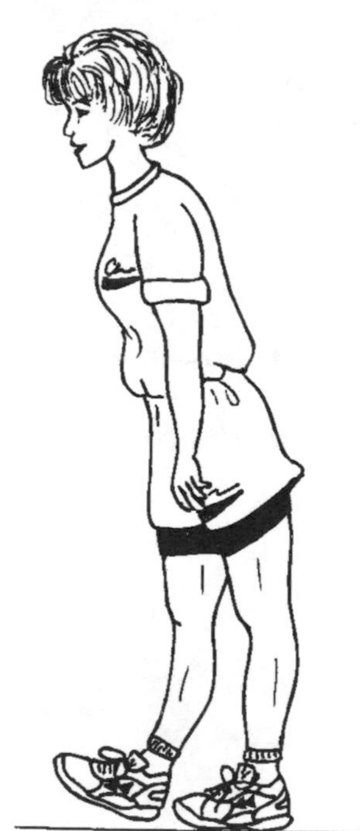

Figure 6.3b

Wrist Strengthening

Wrist strengthening exercises are important for cheering squads that tumble or perform partner stunts and pyramids. The exercises I recommend use a large (#107) rubber band.

All of these strengthening exercises should be utilized as part of your ongoing training program. Not only do they improve strength, but they can also be used to help somcone recuperate after an injury or sustained loss of activity.

Name: **Wrist Extension** (see figure 6.4a)

Starting Position: Seated, making sure knees are flexed to 90-degree angle.

Steps:
1. Grip rubber band with palm down, forearm on thigh.
2. Secure opposite end of rubber band under your foot.
3. Slowly bend wrist up as far as possible.
4. Hold for 3-5 seconds.
5. Lower slowly, keeping forearm on thigh.
6. Do sets of 10 repetitions until comfortably tired.
7. A free weight may be used in place of the rubber band.

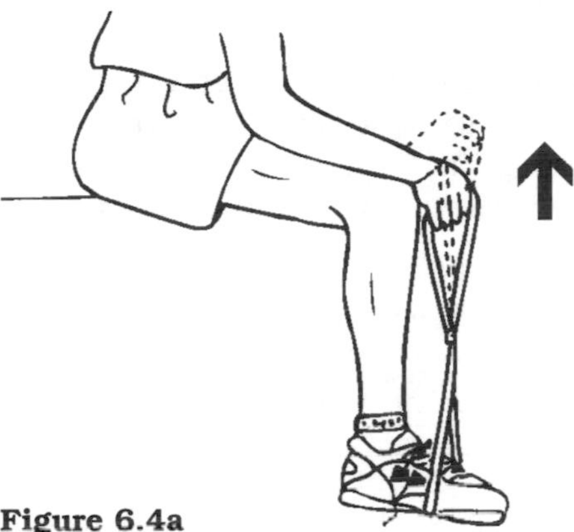

Figure 6.4a

Name: **Wrist Flexion** (see figure 6.4b)

Starting Position: Seated, making sure knees are flexed to 90-degree angle.

Steps:
1. Grip rubber band with palm upward, forearm on thigh.
2. Secure opposite end of rubber band under your foot.
3. Slowly bend wrist up as far as possible.
4. Hold for 3-5 seconds.
5. Lower slowly, keeping forearm on thigh.
6. Do sets of 10 repetitions until comfortably tired.
7. A free weight may be used in place of the rubber band.

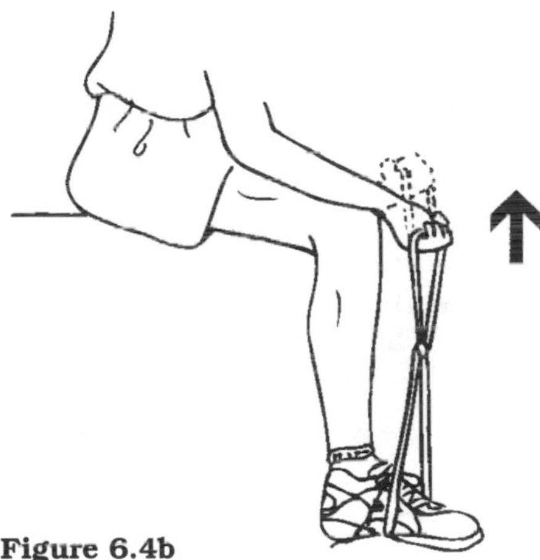

Figure 6.4b

Meeting Time

The end of the practice is a good time to sit down together and get some things organized. There are many things to talk about, and the exact content of this meeting will depend on what needs to get done. Meeting after practice provides you with an excellent opportunity to ask for (and receive) feedback on the different aspects of your program, as well as a time to give positive feedback to your squad about their progress and improvement. Keeping communication lines open will help both you and your cheerleaders fine-tune and nurture the success of the program. Here is a list of possible items that you may discuss at meetings:

- Upcoming pep rally
- Decorating the school for an upcoming game
- Working on a skit
- Talking about uniforms or supplies that need to be ordered
- Planning what cheers to perform at an upcoming game
- Planning new crowd involvement ideas
- Working on a community service project
- Planning or reporting on a fundraising event
- An issue regarding the constitution
- Comments about the quality of the practice and the progress of the skill building
- Communication exercise or group cohesiveness activity
- Preparing for an upcoming competition
- Open discussion about current issues or challenges

THE POSITIVE CIRCLE

I love to end a practice in a Positive Circle. Everyone on the squad (and myself) hooks arms and makes a circle. I start by telling everyone that the purpose of a Positive Circle is to let each person share a short positive statement about how the practice went. Then I tell the squad something that happened during practice that I really feel good about. The next person shares something, and on around the circle until everyone has had a chance to talk. If we are short on time, the Positive Circle changes from statements to single words. I sum up my feelings about the practice with one word, such as "Fantastic!" The next person then shares a word, and we move on around the circle until everyone has shared a word. We end the Positive Circle by saying, "1-2-3, Yes!"

Putting It All Together

If you are a new cheerleading coach, I hope you haven't been overwhelmed by all of the things that go on during a practice. Even though you may have consistent goals and an organized plan for your practice, no two practices will be alike. Some of your practices will be full of numerous activities, and some may specialize in one or two areas. Sometimes you will not be able to follow your plan because of a personal incident (a family tragedy, for instance) and sometimes things just don't run as smoothly as you have planned. My wish for you is that you will remain flexible enough to adapt to changes and focused enough to still be able to meet your goals.

I have devised a basic Daily Practice Schedule for a two-and-one-half-hour practice (see figure 6.5). Of course, you will adjust your times and activities to meet your needs. I think that it's important to allow at least 10 minutes for your cheerleaders to prepare mentally for the practice and to socialize before the work starts. Then I feel you should make a few brief announcements, set goals for the practice, and then maybe share a positive quotation as a theme for the practice. To get the blood flowing to the muscles, have your cheerleaders jog or run around the track or the gym, and follow up with at least 15 minutes of stretching. Select one or two of the strengthening exercises that will benefit your specific skill practice that day (for instance, if you are working on toe touch jumps, do the jump strengthening exercises) and spend at least 10 minutes on them before working about 20 minutes on jumps, stunts, and pyramids. Then you'll need to give a 5-minute break!

After the break, I recommend that you spend at least 30 minutes on your cheers and chants, getting ready for your upcoming events. Follow this session with your aerobic and anaerobic conditioning for about 20 minutes (you'll change the times depending on what you have coming up). Before you start your end-of-practice meeting, have your cheerleaders cool down with light stretching or walking. Your meeting, which may last at

Daily Practice Schedule

Approximate amount of time	*Activity*
10 min	Arrival and preparation
5 min	Announcements, goals, positive quotation
5 min	Warm-up (jog, run)
15 min	Stretching program
10 min	Strengthening exercises
20 min	Jumps, stunts, pyramids
5 min	Break
30 min	Group work: Get ready for upcoming events Chants, cheers, dances (if applicable) Tumbling practice (if applicable)
20 min	Conditioning (aerobic/anaerobic)
5 min	Cooldown (walk and light stretching)
15 min	Meeting Special events, reminders, announcements Unity-building activity, group hug

Figure 6.5 Sample daily practice schedule.

least 15 minutes, can focus on a unity building idea, special events reminders, and discussion on skill development.

Many cheerleading squads practice at least three times a week. I have provided a sample Weekly Practice Plan (see figure 6.6) to help you plan your weekly practice goals. No matter what you select for your specific conditioning or strengthening exercises, and no matter what skills you have selected to work on, there are two areas that are consistent with each practice: the warm-up and the stretch. They precede everything.

An ongoing conditioning program is important for cheerleaders to be able to perform at their peak level during the school year. I have provided a sample Conditioning Program that encompasses all of the cheerleading developmental skill areas (see figure 6.7). To me, "in season" means during the actual sport season your squad is cheering for during the school year. For instance, in the fall, cheerleaders usually begin by cheering for the football season, followed closely by the basketball season. "Off season" means those times that your teams are not competing, such as summer months or after winter sports are finished. Cheerleaders who are faithful to a conditioning program come to practice physically prepared to cheer.

Fun and Effective Practices

In over 25 years of working with cheerleaders, I have collected and experienced many different ideas that help keep practice sessions effective and fun at the same time. As you develop your own program, you may want to refer to these ideas and try those that you are comfortable with. Since the practice session is the heart of your program, you will want to constantly evaluate new ideas on how to improve. Some of these ideas take more time and energy, but the results justify the effort.

1. Always start on time.
2. Validate the behavior you want to

Weekly Practice Plan
Based on 3 practices a week

	Warm-up	Stretch	Condition	Strengthen	Skill	Meeting
	Jog or run	Neck Arms Shoulders Back Trunk Hamstring Groin, hip Quads Abdominal Calf/ankle	*Aerobic:* Run Walk Bike Routine *Anaerobic:* Sprint Jog Walk	*Arms/Legs:* V-lifts Push-ups Tuck jumps Toe raises *Other:* Ankle Wrist	Motions Cheers Chants Dances Tumbling Pyramids Jumps	Spirit Funds Service Unity Misc.
Day 1	5 min	15 min	Anaerobic 15 min	10 min	30 to 45 min	15 min
Day 2	5 min	15 min	Aerobic 15 min	10 min	30 to 45 min	15 min
Day 3	5 min	15 min	Anaerobic 15 min	10 min	30 min	15 min

Figure 6.6 Sample weekly practice plan.

continue ("thank you for being dressed and ready to go so quickly").

3. Make your cheerleaders feel special by smiling, saying their names, talking to each one, complimenting.
4. Be organized. Have a posterboard with the practice schedule listed on it. Keep everything moving.
5. Student leadership will improve your program. Involve all squad members by rotating practice responsibilities. Everyone can learn to take a leadership position on the squad. Rotating leadership during practices builds skill, attitude, participation, and character.
6. Have a motivational quotation on display during practice.
7. Surprise the squad with fruit, nutritious snacks, or beverages.
8. Periodically during a practice, stop and compliment or validate something that is going well (or where you see improvement).
9. Surprise your squad by filming them periodically at practice. The improvement and progression make a fun video for later.
10. When practicing for game cheering, read "game situations" they will find themselves responding to; have them quickly select the appropriate cheer or chant and perform it.
11. Bring a tape recording of a loud crowd responding to a game. After the squad practices a cheer, chant, dance routine, or pyramid, play the tape.
12. Make a Skill Progression Chart (see chapter 5) and a Goal Chart (see chapter 3) on posterboard so they can check off accomplishments.
13. Use music for warm-ups, stretching, and conditioning exercises.

Conditioning Program

	In Season	*Off Season*
Warm-Up	Each practice	Each workout
Stretching Program	3 times a week	3 times a week
Strengthening (jumps/ankles/wrists)	3 times a week	Twice a week if not involved in sports
Aerobic Conditioning (20-30 minutes)	3 times a week	3 to 5 times a week
Anaerobic Conditioning (sprint/jog/walk)	3 times a week	
Jumps	3 to 4 times a week	Once a week after stretching
Accuracy Drills Skill Practice Individual Practice of Basics	At practices when needed	Once a week
If Applicable: Partner Stunts Pyramids Dances Tumbling	At each practice	As needed, depending on program

Figure 6.7 Sample conditioning program.

14. Practice jumps in a circle.
15. Have a surprise creativity session where you divide your cheerleaders into small groups to make up new cheers and chants. Some variations:
    - Pull words out of a hat and use them to make up new cheers and chants
    - Set a theme and redo existing cheers and chants along this theme
    - Make cheers into chants and chants into cheers
16. Give out fun "awards" at the end of practice, such as Best Smile, Most Improved, Attitude Award, Dedication Award, Comedy Award.
17. Do not compare cheerleaders to each other. Individually meet with your cheerleaders to discuss potential, goals, and attitude.
18. Ask a team coach to stop by and give your squad words of encouragement.
19. Appreciate individual and group effort.
20. Always end practice at the time you said it would end.

UNDER THE LIGHTS AT ARROWHEAD

As the director of the professional coed cheerleading squad for the Kansas City Chiefs, I enjoyed four years of working with the best cheerleaders in the country. We would practice at Arrowhead Stadium on Friday nights and Saturday mornings. My favorite times were our late-night practices in the middle of the football field, cheering under the stars, and the huge bank of lights overhead. The stadium was empty and dark, but in our hearts we could hear the roar of the crowd and feel the excitement of the game.

Addressing Body Image

Some athletes are prone to developing eating disorders, and since you spend a lot of time with your cheerleaders at practices and events, you should have a basic knowledge about eating disorders. The two most prevalent disorders are anorexia nervosa and bulimia nervosa.

Anorexia nervosa is characterized by an intense fear of becoming overweight and a disturbance of body image. People experiencing anorexia are afraid of becoming fat and will literally starve themselves to ensure that they do not look overweight. They do not have an accurate picture of their own physical body.

Bulimia nervosa is an eating disorder characterized by a binge-purge syndrome. It also is distinguished by an overconcern about body weight. It involves the ingestion of food (sometimes in unhealthy quantities) followed by purging that includes vomiting, use of laxatives or diuretics, and/or excessive exercise.

As a coach, you should know the warning signs for both so that, if necessary, you are able to help one of your cheerleaders seek professional help.

Warning Signs for Anorexia Nervosa

- ✓ Refusal to eat
- ✓ Dieting even when underweight
- ✓ Hiding body with baggy clothes
- ✓ Amenorrhea (cessation of menstrual periods)
- ✓ Maintaining less than 85 percent of medically healthy weight
- ✓ Obsessing about meal plans and keeping calorie journals
- ✓ Eating in ritualistic ways
- ✓ Exercising compulsively
- ✓ Becoming socially isolated

Warning Signs for Bulimia Nervosa

- ✓ Eating large amounts of food quickly
- ✓ Disappearing after meals or snacks
- ✓ Exhibiting excessive concern about weight. Actual weight may fluctuate, but for a majority of athletes, it will be within their normal range.
- ✓ Alternating between binge-eating and fasting
- ✓ Trying to undo binges by vomiting, fasting, abusing laxatives or diuretics
- ✓ Depression, guilt, and shame following a binge
- ✓ Becoming secretive about eating habits

Do not try to diagnose or treat cheerleaders with any of these symptoms. Since an eating disorder is a very complex problem, help the athlete identify and contact an eating disorders specialist for professional screening. An eating disorder is both a psychological and physiological problem. Diagnoses should be made by a physician, psychologist, and nutritionist trained in eating disorders.

One of your most important responsibilities as a cheerleading coach is to encourage proper nutrition and healthy habits. If you do not have ready access to nutrition information, ask a local dietitian to make a presentation to your squad about healthy habits and proper nutrition for athletes. You could also collect articles from magazines, books, and professional journals to give to your cheerleaders about the nutritional needs of athletes. Another interesting way to educate your cheerleaders is to invite a local, regional, or national athlete (or health professional) to give a talk to your squad about healthy habits.

I feel that it is important for you not to set a weight and height requirement for tryouts. Also, do not have weigh-ins or overemphasize the thinness of individual squad members. Your cheerleaders need to know that you value conditioning, strengthening, endurance, skill development, and crowd leadership as being more important than body size.

You may want to discuss the issue of proper nutrition and healthy habits at one of your parent meetings so they will know what you expect. You could ask them to help you validate healthy habits at home and at school, and to discourage "junk food." Also remember to discuss the warning signs for both anorexia nervosa and bulimia nervosa with the parents of your cheerleaders.

If you would like additional information about eating disorders, please contact the following:

The United States Olympic Committee
Division of Sports Medicine
One Olympic Plaza
Colorado Springs, CO 80909
719-578-4546

American Anorexia/Bulimia Association, Inc. (AABA)
418 E. 76th St.
New York, NY 10021
212-734-1114

Anorexia Nervosa and Related Eating Disorders, Inc. (ANRED)
P.O. Box 5102
Eugene, OR 97405
503-344-1144

Summary

Here are the key points to consider as you are preparing for practices:

- Regularly scheduled and required practice sessions are crucial to building the physical skills required in cheerleading.
- The stretching program should include all major muscle groups and will be more effective if preceded by a general body warm-up.
- Aerobic and anaerobic conditioning will not only improve cheerleading performance but also overall health.
- Strengthening exercises can prevent injuries and improve performance.
- A good practice session should include warm-up, stretching, conditioning, strengthening, skill building, and a squad meeting.
- Institute a year-round conditioning program for your cheerleaders.
- There are many ways to make your practices effective and fun, such as a Skill Progression and Goal Chart, surprise snacks or beverages, music, and special "awards" like Best Smile, Best Athlete, Most Improved, and Attitude Award.
- As a coach, you need to emphasize and encourage proper nutrition and healthy habits.
- There are specific warning signs for anorexia nervosa and bulimia that you should know, since some athletes are prone to disordered eating.

Part III

Coaching Cheerleading Skills

Chapter 7

Basics for Individuals

As in other athletic pursuits, cheerleading requires the mastery of specific individual skills. I will describe such basic skills for cheerleaders as body position and placement, plus how to develop precision, timing, and uniformity. I will also explain proper voice techniques, jumps for cheerleaders, and basic tumbling. A solid foundation in basic, individual skills will provide your cheerleaders with the "raw materials" with which to develop their maximum potential as well as supply the maximum impact for your squad.

Cheering Basics

Cheerleaders lead their crowd by using hand positions, arm positions, and leg positions to execute sideline chants during the game as well as cheers at pregame, halftime, or time outs. As the body moves, it accentuates words. There is a specific place for each body position for each word or beat in a cheer or chant. (Some people confuse the terms "cheer" and "chant": a cheer is performed when the ball is not in play, is longer than a chant, and may feature stunts [pyramids or tumbling]; a chant is a short phrase of words executed along the sidelines in response to a specific game action.)

I will start with a description of the basic body positions, and then give some suggestions on how to develop precision and timing. After cheerleaders master the basic hand, arm, and leg positions, they not only can use their body to lead the crowd more effectively, but can also progress to more advanced athletic skills such as perfect squad synchronization. Not only will your job be easier and the cheerleading more effective if your squad masters these basics, but the respect level for your cheerleaders will be elevated to athlete status.

Hand Positions

Good hand positioning enhances cheerleading effectiveness because the hand, as an extension of the arm, accentuates motions that lead the crowd. The hand position should further define the motion and not detract from it. The four basic hand positions are the fist, the blade, the clap, and the clasp.

With the fist, the thumbs are tightly wrapped on the outside of the fingers. I have seen cheerleaders put their thumbs inside their fingers; from a professional standpoint this should not be done. Putting the thumb inside the fingers doesn't look as strong and also feels awkward. The thumb should not stick out over the edge of the knuckles because the motion again doesn't look as strong and if the thumb sticks out it detracts from the fist motion (see figure 7.1). The wrist for fists and blades should never bend but should always be kept level (a wrist bent upward with open fingers is called a "jazz hand"). A wrist that is bent is called a "broken wrist" if bent upward or downward (or, for downward, sometimes a "puppy dog"). Avoid broken wrists. The three basic fist positions are the dagger, with thumbs facing each other and knuckles upward (see figure 7.2a); the candlestick, with thumbs facing each other and knuckles outward (see figure 7.2b); and the bucket, with thumbs facing downward (see figure 7.2c). These fist positions are paired with arm positions.

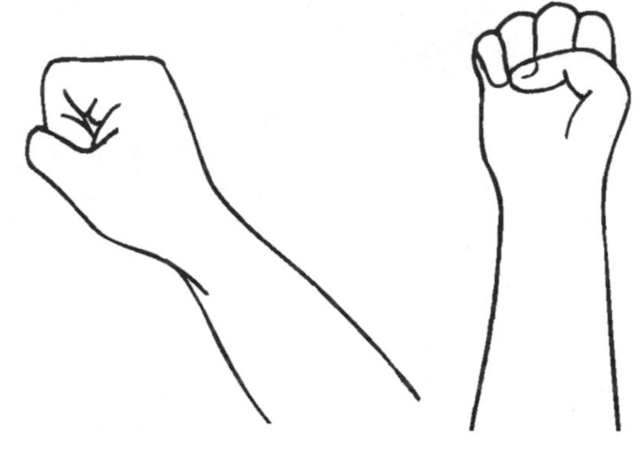

Figure 7.1 The fist: two views.

The blade is the open hand position. The fingers are held tightly together, with the thumb held tightly next to the forefinger. The wrist is kept level (see figure 7.3). When blades are used close to the body, the palms face inward; when blades are used away from the body, the palms face outward.

The other two basic hand positions are the clap and the clasp. The clap is done with the hands held in the blade position when hitting each other (see figure 7.4a). In the clasp, the thumbs and fingers wrap around each other so that the fingers stay together and wrap around the fingers of the other hand while thumbs cross (see figure 7.4b). The clap and the clasp can either be loud or silent, depending on the cheer or chant.

Arm Positions

Cheerleading motions communicate the words of the cheer or chant. The arm positions add emphasis to the message. There are many basic arm positions and the combinations are endless. One arm can do one

Figure 7.2 Three basic fist positions. (a) The dagger. (b) The candlestick. (c) The bucket.

Figure 7.3 The blade.

a b

Figure 7.4 Two basic hand positions. (a) The clap. (b) The clasp.

motion and the other arm can do a totally different motion (some motions are symmetrical and some are not). (Remember that the hands can either be in a fist or a blade for any of these positions.)

The following basic arm positions are illustrated in figures 7.5, a-o:

Arms straight down at sides
Fists or hands on hips
High V
Low V
T position
Baby T
Touchdown
Forward punch
Right full diagonal (right arm up)

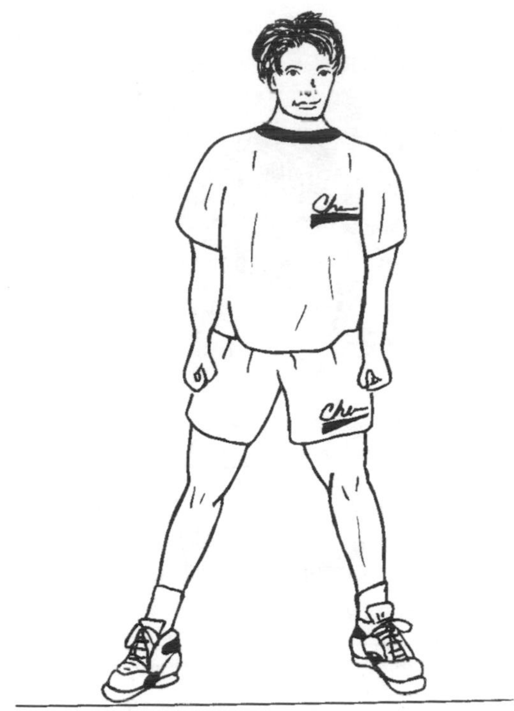

Figure 7.5a Arms straight down at sides.

Figure 7.5b Fists or hands on hips.

Right L (opens right)
Muscle man
Checkmark (low at waist, high over head)
Table top
Indian
Right low angle and left low angle (1/2 low V)

Figure 7.5c High V.

Figure 7.5e T position.

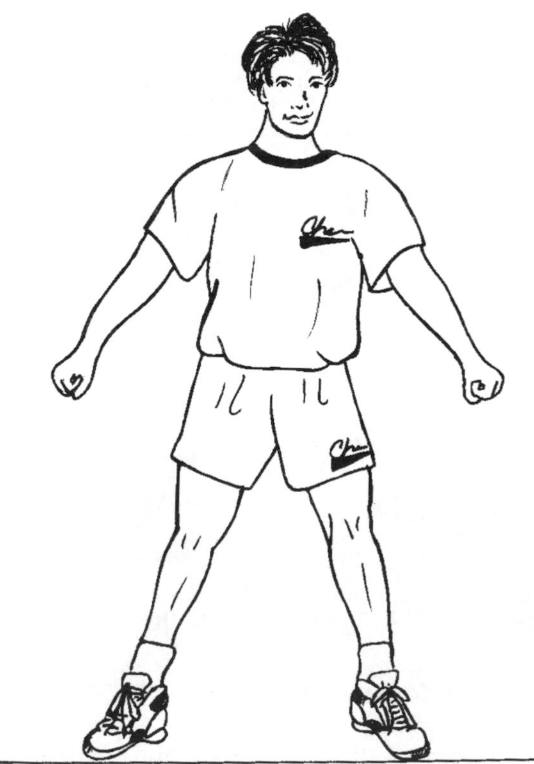

Figure 7.5d Low V.

Figure 7.5f Baby T.

Figure 7.5g Touchdown.

Figure 7.5i Right full diagonal (right arm up).

Figure 7.5h Forward punch.

Figure 7.5j Right L (opens right).

Figure 7.5k Muscle man.

Figure 7.5l Checkmark (low at waist, high over head).

Figure 7.5m Table top.

Figure 7.5n Indian.

Figure 7.5o Right low angle and left low angle (1/2 low V).

Leg Positions

Leg positions in cheers and chants can vary greatly. During sideline chants performed in response to the game action itself, often the legs do not change positions very much because the emphasis is on the arm motions leading the crowd to specific game situation words or phrases. During cheers, cheerleaders will walk around, changing positions, levels, and directions.

I have broken down the leg positions into different categories according to what the legs are doing, and into levels according to the height of the body. For instance, high- to low-level positions would be standing, lunging, kneeling, sitting, and prone or supine. In addition, I will examine kicks and dance moves. As I describe each category, remember that there is room for creativity and combination within each category and between categories.

Standing

In the standing position, the feet can be together or apart, usually shoulder width but sometimes wider. The legs can be straight or both knees can be bent. A "sit" is a position that is a combination of a standing position and a short forward lunge with feet apart, knees bent, and one hip slightly out with weight shifted over the hip. See figures 7.6, a-d for examples of standing positions.

Figure 7.6a Feet together.

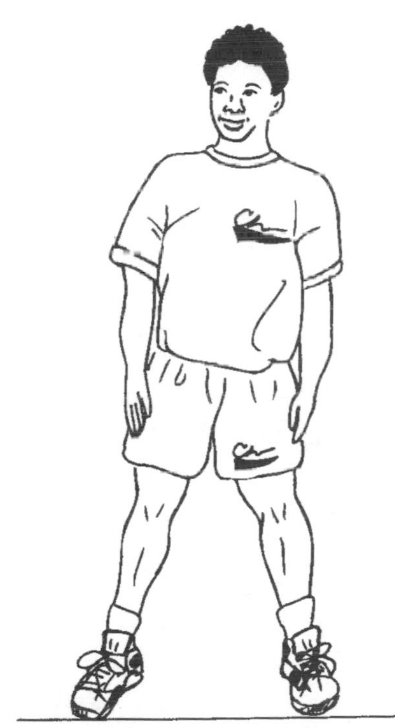

Figure 7.6b Feet apart.

Figure 7.6c Knees bent.

Figure 7.6d Sit.

Walking

Cheerleaders walk forward, backward, and sideways. While walking, they can also cross over (one foot steps over another) and pivot in any direction (one foot is stationary and the other pushes off to make a turn or circle). In the "pop-to" position, the cheerleader hops up and lands with both feet on the floor at the same time, in a variety of leg positions. See figure 7.7, a-b for two walking examples.

Figure 7.7 Walking examples. (a) Walking cross-over. (b) Pop-to position.

Kicks

While kicking is mostly utilized in dancing, cheerleaders use kicks to accentuate part of the words of a cheer or chant or to place the leg in a different location. A kick can be on different levels and in different directions. A kick keeps one foot on the ground at all times, whereas a jump involves both feet off the ground. See figure 7.8, a-b for two kicking examples.

Figure 7.8 Kicking examples.

Lunges

When performing the lunge leg position, one leg is straight and the other leg has a bent knee. In the standing right lunge, the right knee is bent (with knee to foot perpendicular to the floor) and the left leg is straight to the side. In the standing left lunge, the left knee is bent and the right leg is straight to the side. The standing forward lunge is where the knee goes toward the crowd and the straight leg is

Figure 7.9 Lunging examples. (a) Standing right lunge. (b) Standing forward lunge. (c) Standing back step lunge.

in back. In the standing back step lunge, the knee is still toward the crowd, but the straight leg steps back away from the lunge. See figure 7.9, a-c for examples of lunges.

Kneeling

The kneeling leg position means that at least one knee is on the ground. A right kneel means that the right knee is on the ground, with the left knee bent and in line with the left side of the body, left foot on the ground pointed away from the body. The left kneel is just the opposite. The forward kneel means that one knee is on the ground and the other knee and foot are pointed forward. You can also kneel on both knees at the same time. See figure 7.10, a-d for kneeling examples.

Figure 7.10 Kneeling examples. (a) One-knee kneel. (b) Two-knee kneel. (c) Left kneel. (d) Forward kneel.

Sitting

In the sitting position, the legs can be straight out in front, flat on the floor with legs straight, folded Indian style, folded under (sitting on feet), or in a stag position (one leg is bent in front and the other is bent in back). The splits would fall under this category because the level is the same. In the splits, the legs are perpendicular to the body in opposite directions.

Prone or Supine

The body is parallel to the ground with legs straight for these positions. In the prone position, the body is face-down, and in the supine position, the body is face-up. The prone or supine position is sometimes used at the end of a routine for dramatic effect.

Dance Moves

Dance steps are sometimes used in cheers and chants. Dance moves can utilize combinations of all other basic leg positions. They are different from regular cheer motions in that dance moves usually flow from one position to the next. Cheer motions are precise, do not flow, and have a specific position for a specific beat.

Precision, Accuracy, and Timing

Your squad must develop precise and accurate motions if they are going to have good timing. "Precise" means that the motions are tight, crisp, and distinct with the beat or word. "Accurate" means that the motions are executed correctly. "Timing" means a squad of individuals doing the same thing at the same time, which can result from practicing accuracy and precision drills.

Here are some coaching suggestions on how you can help your cheerleaders learn how to develop strong motions.

Accuracy Drills

One way to build precision and timing in cheerleading motions is to practice accuracy drills that use the different hand, arm, and leg positions. An accuracy drill is a set of cheerleading movements that flows from one position to another to a specific beat. Each drill consists of one eight-count sequence, with each beat having a particular position. The accuracy drill itself usually consists of four to eight eight-counts done in a row.

The Accuracy Drill

Purpose. To practice hand, arm, and leg motions used in cheers and chants.

Procedure. You and your cheerleaders make up four eight-count drills comprised of motions that you use in your cheers and chants. Teach them to the rest of the squad and practice hitting the motions with precision and uniformity.

Coaching Points. The emphasis is on precision—tight motions, specific placement, having a definite stop after each beat. After your cheerleaders master the basic arm motions, you do not need to use an accuracy drill. This drill can be practiced individually in front of a mirror or in small groups. When learning the names of the arm positions, the cheerleaders can say the name of the motion instead of counting, such as "High V, Low V, Baby T, Checkmark," or they can count each beat aloud.

Variation. Another way to create an accuracy drill for new cheerleaders is to put together sequences of motions from cheers and chants that your school uses, but without the words for these beginning practices. The cheerleaders will focus on the motions more if the words come later. Refer to the sample eight-count sequence that can be used as an accuracy drill to get you started (see figure 7.11, a-i).

Precision and Timing Drills

There are specific drills and practice procedures that you can use to help your cheerleaders improve their precision and timing. Try as many of the following as possible.

Stop and Check

Purpose. To improve the precision of individual motions.

Procedure. Decide on a specific cheer or chant to perform as a group. Have your cheerleaders stop at every beat or every word to check everyone's motions.

Coaching Points. Look for consistency in angles, lines, levels, and body positions.

Line Up

Purpose. To work on squad timing and motion transition.

Procedure. Line up your cheerleaders in groups of three. These drills can be done standing shoulder to shoulder or lined up

(continued)

Figure 7.11 The Accuracy Drill. (a) Fist on hips, clap 5-6-7-8. (b) Table top. (c) High V. (d) Left L. (e) Full left diagonal. (f) Touchdown. (g) Right high V in lunge position. (h) Left high V in lunge position. (i) Low V.

Figure 7.11 *(continued)*

behind each other. Call out the following motion sequences: (1) high V, low V; (2) T, baby T; (3) right lunge, stand, left kneel; (4) pivot, kick.

Coaching Points. Look for consistent angles in high V, low V, parallel lines in T, baby T; consistent levels in right lunge, stand, left kneel; and controlled body positions and smoothness in pivot, kick.

Motion Drill

Purpose. To make sure everyone knows the names of the motions and can hit the motions at the same time.

Procedure. Have a list of basic motions to refer to, and then call out a motion for everyone to hit. After you say "touchdown" you want your squad to hit the touchdown motion and say the word "touchdown" at the same time.

Coaching Points. Emphasize that timing is very important to the execution of your cheers and chants and that motion drills can help the squad improve. Watch for consistency in angles, lines, levels, and body positions. If possible, videotape this session so that squad members can see their progress.

Count It Out

Purpose. To practice accurate, precise motions while doing a short accuracy drill.

Procedure. Have individuals or pairs take turns practicing the following short accuracy drill. The cheerleaders count during the drill, hitting the motion on the number. Count out "5-6-7-8," clapping once as you call each number. This will get everyone together to start the following motions: (1) touchdown, (2) right L, (3) baby T, (4) low V, (5) left diagonal, (6) table top, (7) high V, (8) fists on hips.

Coaching Points. Watch for consistency, accuracy, precision, and timing. You should be able to tell who needs extra help on their motions from this session. Be sure to set up additional practices on motion precision and timing if your squad cannot perform this accuracy drill with a high level of accomplishment.

These are other ideas for developing precision and timing on your squad:

- Practice in front of mirrors or windows so everyone can see everyone else.
- Use actual game action chants to practice squad timing.

- Pair up an experienced cheerleader with a novice cheerleader and have them work together.
- Ask a collegiate cheerleader or professional cheerleading instructor to lead accuracy practice.
- Watch a national cheerleading competition on TV and discuss precision, timing, technique, and transition of arm and leg movements.

Not only will your job be easier and the cheerleading more effective if your squad masters these basics, but the respect level for your cheerleaders will be elevated to athlete status.

Proper Voice Technique

The voice can make a difference. Voice inflection, volume, pitch, and expression are powerful crowd leadership tools. How the words are conveyed during the cheers and chants can have a dramatic impact on the total effectiveness of your cheerleading squad. Here's how these tools are used in cheerleading and a suggestion on how you can coach proper voice technique.

Inflection

Inflection is the accent on specific words, the beat of a cheer or chant. Proper inflection lets the crowd know what to yell in support of the team during the game. If you were doing a chant, "Go Big Red," you would have your cheerleaders emphasize each word equally, with a pause after "Red," so that you have four beats: "Go Big Red" (pause). The pause can be a clap to keep the beat going. If you were working on the chant "Let's Go Big Red Let's Go," your inflection would be on the two "Go"s and you would have either one clap or two fast claps to keep the beat after the last "Go": "Let's *Go* Big Red Let's *Go*" (clap-clap). With inflection and claps to keep beats, you can train your cheerleaders to lead the crowd more effectively. When working with your cheerleaders on this concept, you may want to illustrate what you mean by using a simple inflection bar graph drawing (figure 7.12).

Volume

Volume is how loud the voice sounds. Game action words and wimpy voices don't mix. Breathing needs to be from the diaphragm. Check to make sure your cheerleaders are breathing deeply to help amplify the sound (many cheerleaders simply use the small amount of air in the throat instead of all of the air in the lungs). At an early practice, ask each cheerleader to say a chant as if they were cheering at a game and check for volume. Practice with one-syllable words such as "go" or "ha" to get the air going and raise the volume. Coach your cheerleaders to focus on projecting their voices across the gym or across the field by using the air in the lungs. Have them put their hands on their stomachs to feel the difference between shallow breathing from the throat and deep breathing from the diaphragm. The more they can use the diaphragm, the louder the words will sound. The words need to be heard for effective leadership.

Pitch

Pitch is whether the voice is high or low. Excited vocal chords vibrate faster, causing high pitched sounds. Not only does this sound terrible, but high voices do not carry very far. Cheerleaders run the risk of hurting their vocal chords if they use shallow breathing and yell from high pitched voices.

Go	Big	Red	(clap)
1	2	3	4

Let's	GO	Big	Red	Let's	GO	(clap)	(clap)
1	2	3	4	5	6	7	8

Figure 7.12 Inflection bar graph.

Lower pitched voices sound better, are easier to listen to, carry farther, and are stronger, more commanding. Have your cheerleaders say the words together in their natural speaking voices, and sometimes at a little lower pitch (but not *too* low or awkward sounding). Use a tape recorder to allow your cheerleaders to hear the difference between high pitched voices and low pitched voices, and spend some time early in the season to focus on lower voices.

Expression

Expression is the emotion in the voice. It's a combination of pitch, volume, and inflection expressed with individual style. It's how the personality comes through. Have your cheerleaders practice the words to the cheers as if they *really* mean it! I once observed a squad that used delightful expression and personality when they cheered the name of their team: the Rough Raiders. They rolled the "r" in a slight growl, which grabbed the crowd's attention.

Have your cheerleaders practice how they will say the words in the cheers and chants. Make sure everyone says all of the words (sometimes cheerleaders are so involved in the motions that they forget to say the words—don't let them get by with this). Evaluate each person's inflection, volume, pitch, and expression. The words should never sound phony (affected), overdone, wimpy, garbled, sing-song, mush-mouthed, or cutesy. Your cheerleaders should sound natural yet commanding, loud yet expressive, and definitely easy to understand.

Many coaches and cheerleading squads do not practice the effective use of vocal communication and leadership. Since the primary responsibility of your cheerleaders is to lead the crowd during athletic events, be sure to stress the importance of these four words: *low, loud, clear, expressive.*

During practices, isolate the words (practice them without motions) with particular attention to low pitch (but not a forced or unnatural sounding lowness), loud and unified volume (use plenty of air but do not screech), and clear enunciation of words (make sure words are distinct and do not run into each other). The expression in your cheerleaders' voices should build excitement and command attention. Here's an example of what you can do at practice.

Coaching Voice Technique

When you are coaching your cheerleaders, remember that voices can make a lot of difference in the overall effectiveness of your squad. Make voice practice a valuable part of your training program. I have devised a Voice Technique Evaluation Form (figure 7.13) that can be utilized during practices and games. You may want to ask other faculty members or administrators to fill out one of these forms early in the season to see if your cheerleaders are on track. The form can be used for individuals as well as for the entire squad cheering at once. This evaluation can help isolate some problem areas, and also help validate effective voice technique. After your cheerleaders have made a habit of cheering with effective voices, you won't need to use the form any longer. Remember to discuss voice techniques with your prospective cheerleaders before tryouts.

Voice Technique Practice

Purpose. To develop inflection, volume, pitch, and expression in your cheerleaders' voices.

Procedure. On separate pieces of posterboard, write the words to a few of your squad's favorite cheers and chants. Explain to the squad that you are concerned about the effectiveness of their verbal communication. Hold up one posterboard at a time for the squad to say the words of the cheer or chant together.

Coaching Points. You want voices that are low and loud yet natural sounding. If the voices are high, screeching, or annoying, have your cheerleaders breathe deeper (use more air), lower their voices a little, and project the words across the room. The words should be clearly enunciated. Ask your cheerleaders to slow down to enunciate and be more precise in word formation if you cannot easily understand them. You want voices that are expressive and exciting. If your cheerleaders sound dull, boring, or lackluster, relate a game action situation that is charged with emotion and have your cheerleaders repeat the cheer or chant like they really mean it, with fire and energy.

Jumps

Jumps are very important in the athletic world of cheerleading, and they take more

Voice Technique Evaluation Form

Directions: A ✓ means "work needed" and a ★ means "good job."

Inflection

____ Accent on specific words; the beat
____ Clear enunciation; easy to understand
____ Distinct words

Volume

____ Loudness
____ Unified volume
____ Breathing from diaphragm

Pitch

____ Low intonation
____ Full, not shallow
____ Sound natural

Expression

____ Emotion, energy, personality
____ Words come alive; excitement
____ Command leadership

Figure 7.13 Voice technique evaluation form.

practice than just about anything else to master. Above all else, I believe that you can evaluate the skill level of a cheerleading squad by the quality of their jumps. Good jumps command attention and respect (there's something about being airborne that fascinates people). They supply the power source, the electricity, the excitement on the sidelines. A jump is energy personified. It communicates without words. A jump further reinforces cheerleaders as athletes because of the exceptional skill required to perform one.

Stretching, strengthening, and conditioning are extremely important to the mastery of excellent jumps. These areas are covered in chapter 6. In this chapter, I will discuss jump prerequisites, jump execution, specific single jumps, combination jumps, and productive jump practice.

Prerequisites

As the cheerleading coach, you need to understand a few basics before you begin to incorporate jumps into your program. First of all, it's extremely important that you make sure your cheerleaders thoroughly stretch before each jump practice. A conditioning program that includes both anaerobic and aerobic exercises will help develop the stamina and body control essential in jumping, and strengthening exercises will improve the execution of specific jumps. All three of these topics—stretching, conditioning, and strengthening—were presented in chapter 6. They provide the foundation for achieving your goal of beautiful jumps.

Since jumps require a lot of hard work, it is important to request an individual commitment from each cheerleader to set specific goals for accomplishment. Make sure your cheerleaders, after they have set their goals, proceed from beginning jumps to intermediate jumps before attempting the more difficult jumps. You may want to make a Jump Progression and Accomplishment Chart to keep track of individual progress (see figure 7.14).

Your cheerleaders need to jump (and cheer) in athletic shoes with good foot and ankle support. Since ankle injury is the number

Jump Progression and Accomplishment Chart

Name of cheerleader ____________________

✓ = Beginning level + = Improvement ★ = Mastery

Jump Progression	Aug. 30	Sept. 15	Sept. 30	Oct. 15	Oct. 30	Nov. 15	Nov. 30
Spread eagle							
Herkie							
Stag							
Hurdler							
Toe touch							

Figure 7.14 Jump progression and accomplishment chart.

one cheerleader injury, your squad's shoe selection is very important.

Jump Execution

Jump execution means the entire jumping procedure from beginning to end. The jump starts with the prep and ends with the clean-up. I will go through the basic procedure for the execution of a basic jump, listing hints for each step. Work on the sequence of prep, whip, lift, land, and clean-up with specific jumps described later in the chapter. You can build greater power and stamina if you practice the strengthening exercises in chapter 6. Also, refer to the accompanying illustrations. You must understand the entire procedure for how to execute a jump to coach your cheerleaders in jump development.

The Prep

Each jump is preceded by a "prep," which means that you prepare to do the jump by a sequence of body positions that lead up to the jump. A long prep will give you less energy to perform the actual jump and is not necessary. A standardized prep will enable your squad members to incorporate jumps into cheers and chants with good timing. Start with the arms in a high V, feet together and weight on the balls of the feet. Focus high and keep your shoulders back and relaxed. Preceding the jump, have a squad member call "5-6-7-8" to establish a unified beat for perfect timing.

The Whip

Following the call, whip your arms around in front of the body, bending at the knees but staying on the balls of the feet. Keep your focus high and your shoulders back and relaxed.

The Lift

Circle the arms around, lift from the shoulders, and hit the desired jump. When jumping, obtain your maximum height first and then whip the legs to the various positions. At the height of the jump, toes should be pointed, arms stiff and controlled, and head up.

The Landing

Land lightly, with feet together, on the balls of your feet with knees bent. Arms should be in a T position for the landing. The landing of a jump takes a downward whipping motion by the legs in order for the feet to land together. Land toes-to-heel, absorbing the weight with bent knees. To polish off the jump, slap the hands at your sides. Head should still be up. This is a recovery time if feet didn't land together, or if timing was off in the group.

The Clean-Up

As a final step, stand up with the feet apart and place hands in a fist position on your hips for a clean, polished ending.

SPECIFIC JUMPS

- **Spread Eagle:** Legs are spread to a straddle position with toes pointed (see figure 7.15a). Arms can form either a high V, a T, above the head clasp, or touchdown position.
- **Herkie:** One leg is straight to the side while the other bends at the knee. The bent knee either faces the floor or to the front (see figure 7.15b). Arms are usually in a T or touchdown position.
- **Stag Sit:** One leg is extended in a toe touch position and one is bent at the knee in a stag position (see figure 7.15c). Arms can copy the legs, or go to a touchdown or T position.
- **Abstract:** One leg is bent inward with a stag sit while the other is bent behind with the knee facing down (see figure 7.15d). Arms can be in a T, hands on hips to a sailor salute, or hand flash above the head. This jump is also sometimes used in dance routines.
- **Hurdler:** This jump is similar to the track event. One leg is extended forward while the other is bent at the knee and pulled up in back. Most people prefer to extend the best kicking leg. Arms should whip around the head to aim toward the floor. Keep your chest high. The goal is the maximum extension of the front leg (see figure 7.15e).
- **Double Nine:** Both the arms and legs form nines (or a P, depending on which leg is used). The leg extended in front is level while the opposite leg bends at the knee. The foot of the bent knee should touch the inside knee of the extended leg (see figure 7.15f). This jump requires a whipping motion both on the way up and down in order to land with both feet at the same time. This jump is advanced and requires much practice.
- **Pike:** The object of this advanced jump is to keep the upper body straight and tight

Figure 7.15a Spread eagle.

as the legs are whipped straight out in front. Arms are pulled around in front, parallel with the legs (see figure 7.15g). This jump requires 100 percent energy on the way up as well as down.

- **Toe Touch:** This advanced jump is probably the favorite jump for cheerleaders, requiring extensive practice and energy for perfection. The back, head, and shoulders are upright while tightening the abdomen and relaxing the leg muscles during this jump. It is not important that your toes

Figure 7.15b Herkie.

Figure 7.15c Stag sit.

Figure 7.15d Abstract.

Figure 7.15e Hurdler.

Figure 7.15f Double nine.

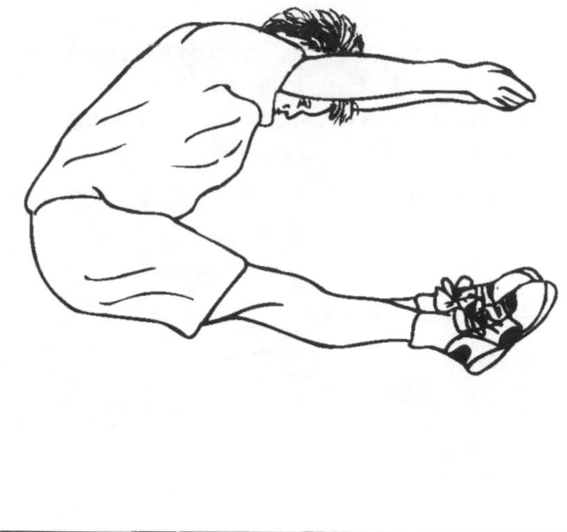

Figure 7.15g Pike.

actually touch your hands (this promotes leaning forward and lowering shoulders which lowers the height of the jump). Keep the arms level in a T position and bring the feet to your hands (see figure 7.15h). Sometimes this jump is called a "Russian," which really describes the position of the arms: both are thrown downward between the legs for another arm variation.

- **Around the World:** Before trying this advanced jump, make sure you have mastered the pike and the toe touch. Start with a pike, and then whip the legs open to the toe touch position (see figure 7.15i). Whipping with the arms as well as legs makes this advanced jump easier.

Jump Combinations

Combinations are two or more different jumps done in succession. A series is the same jump done two or more times in succession. The following are some examples of combination jumps:

- Herkie to toe touch
- Spread eagle to abstract
- Hurdler to toe touch

Jumps are also combined with gymnastics: for instance a back handspring to a toe touch or a round-off to a spread eagle. Jumps into knee drops, seat drops, or splits are definitely not recommended because, according to the National Federation's *High School*

Figure 7.15h Toe touch.

Figure 7.15i Around the world.

Spirit Rules Book, the body should not be airborne before ending in a knee drop, seat drop, or splits. As a coach, you can promote the acquisition of jumping skills by increasing the amount of jumps incorporated into cheers, chants, and routines. It is important when training cheerleaders in jumping to emphasize a strong follow-through and clean ending. The commitment to mastering jumping skills will aid the development of your squad's effectiveness because of the explosive and impressive impact on your crowd.

Productive Jump Practices

The performance of outstanding jumps takes a lot of hard work. I recommend that you begin jump training immediately after tryouts by starting your squad on their strength and conditioning program (see chapter 6) as soon as possible. Extensive and ongoing training is necessary for the development of outstanding jumps. Since practicing jumps is hard work, you'll need to vary your jump practice sessions.

Individual commitment is needed to develop the skills necessary to perform outstanding jumps. Your squad needs to know that you are serious about helping them improve their jumps. Your cheerleaders' overall performance impact will skyrocket if they can execute excellent jumps. I will discuss five different ideas on how to structure jump practices: isolation, circle, contest, add on, and jump-a-thon.

Isolation

Isolate the jump that needs practice. By concentrating on one jump at a time, each cheerleader will be able to reinforce the skill progression for a specific jump through repetition and focus. Try using a video camera. When you film, your cheerleaders will automatically try harder to do a good job, plus watching the tape later is an excellent teaching tool and is usually a lot of fun.

Circle

Practice the jumps in a jump circle. Everyone makes a circle, with one person starting a jump, then the next one in the circle does the same jump, and on around the circle. After you have completed the circle, start again with a different jump. You will be able to quickly assess each person's skill level on each jump. Have your cheerleaders begin with easy jumps and work up to harder jumps. Keep this session moving by having the next cheerleader begin the prep while the preceding jumper is executing the follow-through or landing.

Contest

To build endurance and strength, announce that you are having a continuous jumping contest and have your cheerleaders do sets of five jumps in a row. The goal of the contest is to see who can do five acceptable jumps in the shortest amount of time. Time each person and write down the time and the number of acceptable jumps performed. Continue with sets of five jumps. Announce winners and give awards for endurance, execution, difficulty of jumps, and improvement.

Add On

Play a jumping game called Add On. Begin with one person doing a jump of their choice. The next person does the same jump, and then adds a jump to it. This continues around the jump circle until everyone is "out." (A person is out if the sequence of jumps plus one new jump cannot be completed.)

Jump-a-thon

Another fun way to practice jumps is to have a jump-a-thon. Have your squad members take pledges for how many jumps they can do in a specific amount of time. The jump-a-thon can be held during practice or at another time. Raise money and skill at the same time!

Basic Tumbling

Most cheerleading squads incorporate tumbling skills into their program. The degree of emphasis varies from school to school. Some squads incorporate tumbling into their program simply because they have a gymnast (or many gymnasts) on their squad. Some squads consist of individuals with no tumbling background and all skills are added after the squad starts practicing. Incorporating tumbling into your squad's performance repertoire can add variety, creativity, and excitement to your competition routine, and you can display additional athletic skills during pep rallies and games. There's something about a well-executed tumbling pass that grabs the crowd's attention and electrifies the air.

If you do not have a tumbling or gymnastics background, you need to know these basics:

- Always use mats when working on tumbling skills.
- If your squad wants to tumble, bring in a qualified gymnastics coach to work with your cheerleaders. Some squads go to a gymnastics studio.
- Learn how to spot tumbling from a qualified gymnastics instructor (some schools have a gymnastics program but most schools do not) so that you can practice spotting each other.
- Begin early and allow plenty of time for your squad to master tumbling skills.
- Assess the skill level of each person on your squad and set up a safe progression of tumbling skills to be learned.
- Start with the basics before moving to more advanced skills. A basic progression would be forward roll to backward roll, cartwheel, round-off, walkover (front and back), handstand, limber (front and back), handspring (front and back), round-off back handspring, back tuck.

- Make sure your pre-tryout training sessions, your tryouts, and your judging form reflect the tumbling that is expected.

For additional information, refer to ASEP's *Rookie Coaches Gymnastics Guide* (written in cooperation with USA Gymnastics).

Summary

The following are key points for individuals who are developing cheerleading basics:

- Cheerleaders lead their crowd by using hand, arm, and leg positions that they have practiced and mastered.
- One of the most effective ways to build precision, accuracy, and timing in cheerleading motions is through drills.
- Voice inflection, volume, pitch, and expression are powerful crowd leadership tools.
- Jumps convey the athletic skill of the cheerleading squad.
- A variety of specific jumps can be learned, practiced, and mastered for effective cheering.
- Tumbling skills can be added to your cheerleader program.
- The incorporation of tumbling skills into your program will require specialized coaching knowledge and experience.

Chapter 8

© National Cheerleaders Association 1996

Safety and Stunts

Cheerleaders may stretch, condition, strengthen, and practice basic skills on their own, but they will ultimately work with a group of other cheerleaders—a squad. A squad trains as a team, performing stunts (any mount, pyramid, or tumbling skill) at varying levels of expertise. As the coach of a squad who wants to perform stunts, you may want to know how stunt and safety issues have evolved to where they are now.

Cheerleading is not what it used to be. Safety has not always been a cheerleading issue. Bouncing up and down on the sidelines in ankle-length skirts, yelling for the team, was not very risky to say the least. Over the past few decades, cheerleading has evolved into an athletic expression of both skill and spirit. As cheerleaders have added stunts to their routines, safety issues have developed along a parallel track.

Why has cheerleading become more physical?

- There are many opportunities for cheerleading competition: for instance, summer camp; local, state, or regional events; and national competitions. Cheerleaders incorporate stunts into their routines to create more excitement and gain more points. Many of these competitions adhere to a specific set of safety rules.
- Nationally televised high school and collegiate cheerleading championships have brought advanced stunts into the homes of thousands of cheerleaders who want to achieve the same level of accomplishment.
- A much higher percentage of cheerleaders are female, and traditionally females have not had the same athletic choices males have had. One reason cheerleading became more

physical is that female athletes wanted to push the limit of their abilities and to elevate the reputation of cheerleading to athlete status. Ironically, it was this push to greater athleticism that also attracted males to cheerleading (which offers good opportunities for special stunts).

As cheerleaders became more athletic and began performing more difficult stunts, the chance for injury rose considerably. Incidents of catastrophic injury to cheerleaders are very low compared to other athletes, but a few lawsuits that gained national attention have caused great concern. To some people, injury to a cheerleader was unheard of and unbelievable because cheerleading was not regarded as an athletic activity. However, athletes always run the risk of injury—and cheerleaders are athletes.

As stunts became an integral part of many cheerleading programs, safety issues moved to the forefront—particularly over the past decade—led by the professional cheerleading companies and the National Federation of State High School Associations. Coaches needed help. Middle school or junior high and high school squads wanted to emulate what they saw at collegiate games and on television. They wanted to try something new, to be different and better than preceding squads, and to push the limits of their abilities.

In this chapter, I will discuss safety issues as they relate to the group skills that are necessary to perform mounts and pyramids as well as provide examples of mounts and how to teach them.

Cheerleader Safety

Since cheerleading has evolved into an athletic endeavor, cheerleaders need specific safety guidelines as they begin to add stunts to their routines. Many additional skills are involved with stunts, and the risk of injury is greater. Your responsibility as coach is to create an athlete mindset about stunting so that your squad will understand the seriousness of safety issues. Stunts and safety are to be taught and practiced at the same time.

It is vital that you locate the source of the safety guidelines for your school. Check into existing rules for your league, conference, district, region, county, or city. Also, contact your State High School Association to see what safety rules have been adopted by your state (over 30 states have adopted the safety rules from the National Federation of State High School Associations, which meets each year to review and revise the safety rules). If your area or state does not have safety rules for you to implement, get in touch with the National Federation for their *High School Spirit Rules Book*; it contains safety rules, definitions of terms, photographs illustrating some of the rules and safety issues, sample situations and subsequent rulings, plus other informative articles for coaches. Contact the National Federation at this address for their current rules book and videotapes:

National Federation of State High School Associations
11724 NW Plaza Cir., P.O. Box 20626
Kansas City, MO 64195-0626
816-464-5400

I recommend that you merge your local rules with the National Federation's safety rules. Make sure that your safety rules have been approved by your principal and athletic director.

After you have adopted a set of safety rules, you will need to learn everything about safety, spotting, and stunts that you can. Besides using this book as a resource, you can also attend summer camps, one-day clinics, or workshops. Most of the professional cheerleading companies teach safety rules along with their instruction on spotting, mounts, and pyramids. Another suggestion is to ask a collegiate cheerleader or professional instructor who is knowledgeable about safety, spotting, and stunting procedures to come and work with your squad.

Your next step is to teach the safety rules and stunting procedures to your cheerleaders. If possible, schedule sessions during the summer practices (if you have them) so you can specifically work on safety and spotting. If you do not have summer practices or don't have tryouts until the fall, plan to have these stunt and safety sessions early in the season. Implementing safety rules is one of your most important jobs as cheerleading coach. This chapter will give you the foundation you need. Your hands-on experiences with your squad will help you master these skills.

As your cheerleaders gain experience and confidence in building mounts and pyramids, you will need to continue to monitor the safety procedures. Some cheerleading squads do not think they need to follow the rules (or that they need a spotter). Continually validate the safety rules. I verbally reinforce good spotting, bring posterboard charts to each practice with the rules illustrated and explained, review safety issues during practice as we are building stunts, and, if I don't remember a specific detail about a safety or stunt issue, I look it up and we discuss the issue as a squad. I want my cheerleaders to know that if in doubt, we should check it out!

TAKING RESPONSIBILITY FOR YOUR OWN SAFETY

Sometimes cheerleaders know the rules but decide not to follow them. On one squad I was working with one girl who didn't want to take out her diamond post earring. During practice, the earring was accidentally ripped out of her ear during a stunt, causing a high level of pain and a hard-to-heal injury. During another session with a different squad, a girl was injured because she tried a stunt without the proper spotter. You need to impress upon your cheerleaders that the rules are to be followed in all cases, and they should monitor their own as well as others' safety at all times.

Over the past decade, there have been a few critical injuries to cheerleaders. Diligence and commitment to safety will reduce the possibilities of injuries. Your cheerleaders need safety guidelines—and they need for you to locate, learn, teach, implement, and monitor these safety guidelines. Safety education provides the foundation from which athletes may develop. It's up to you to make it happen.

General Safety Guidelines

To help you establish a solid foundation of safety education, I will give you an overview of the basic safety issues to consider: practice location, stunt considerations, spotting, and personal appearance guidelines.

Practice Location

Make sure your practices are held in a location that provides the greatest safety to your cheerleaders. I recommend a wooden floor, such as a basketball court. You do not want a lot of outside noise to distract your cheerleaders. And be sure to remove any obstructions, such as gym class equipment. Keep megaphones, pompons, and crowd involvement signs out of the way until they are actually used. Personal items should be placed away from the practice area. Do not allow visitors to your practice sessions.

Stunt Considerations

If your squad performs stunts, use mats until the stunts are mastered. Do not let your cheerleaders perform or practice stunts on concrete, on wet or uneven surfaces, or in a space that is crowded, not well lit, or has obstructions or obstacles close-by. Tumbling should never be performed over or under a mount or pyramid. And remind cheerleaders never to participate in stunts when the ball is in play. Since they are dangerous and have been the cause of catastrophic injury, minitrampolines (or anything that can propel a cheerleader) should never be used.

When you are working with your cheerleaders on mounts and pyramids, do not allow them to build any higher than two levels (refer to "two high" in the following definitions). You can easily check this by making sure that anyone whose feet are off the ground is being supported by someone whose feet are on the ground. Also, watch for how your cheerleaders dismount (come down) after a mount or pyramid. If someone is shoulder height or above, the landing should be assisted. You can teach your cheerleaders to assist landings by having the base person maintain hand-to-hand contact with the top person all the way to the cheering surface.

Spotting

The spotter is the most important person on your squad, the guardian of safety. The responsibility of the spotter is to watch for safety hazards such as weight shifting, an unstable base position or unstable top person, or inadequate knowledge of the stunt. The spotter must be in a position to prevent injuries, particularly to the head, neck, and back areas. The spotter makes it possible for your squad to be able to learn new mounts safely and to develop further athletic abilities.

Spotting is taught at the same time the stunt is taught. Even though the spotter is not directly involved in the actual stunt, a good spotter understands the proper positioning of both the base person and top person. This knowledge of the actual stunt procedure will enable the spotter to assist the stunt during learning and practicing, plus protect the safety of the top person. The coach must also understand proper spotting procedures in order to teach, demonstrate, and assist. You can further your stunt and safety education by attending coach conventions, summer camp, by working with professional instructors or college cheerleaders, or by asking an experienced coach in your area to help you. Your attitude and example will validate the seriousness of the responsibility.

The following four tips for spotters will give you the basics that you and your squad members need to know about safety and spotting.

FOUR TIPS FOR SPOTTERS

1. **Stay Close**
   Use hands-on spotting (touching the stunters) during the learning process. Always stand close to the stunt. The actual location of the spotter depends upon the procedure for building the stunt and where the spotter can advantageously see the head/neck areas of the top person. The most important areas to spot are the head, neck, and shoulder areas. Don't walk away from the stunt until after the dismount.

2. **Stay Alert**
   Maintain visual contact with the top person at all times. Keep quiet to hear a possible "down" call by the top person or base person. Stay mentally focused on the stunt being performed.

3. **Be Ready**
   Be able to shift positions to counteract movements of the top person. Watch where the hips shift. The spotter's actual location will depend on how the stunt is being built (for most beginning and intermediate stunts, this is to the side or at a 45-degree angle). Stand with feet apart, hands up. Focus on protecting the head, neck, and shoulder area.

4. **Respond to Emergency**
   Be prepared to break the fall of the top person by wrapping around the waist, shoulders, or scooping under the arms. Always protect the head and neck area. Don't try to force the stunt to stay up.

Make sure that your cheerleaders use spotters until a stunt is mastered. Each cheerleader on your squad should have experience serving as spotter. Do not recruit someone not on the squad to come to practice to help spot! Spotting is serious and should be treated with the utmost respect.

Personal Appearance Guidelines

The personal appearance of your cheerleaders will influence their safety as well as the impact of their performance. For both appearance and safety reasons, your cheerleaders should not wear jewelry. My opinion is that personal jewelry detracts from the uniform and the uniformity of the squad, while at the same time causes a safety hazard to the wearer and others. Long fingernails can also cause a safety hazard, so I recommend an athletic length, which is not beyond the fingertip.

Cheerleaders should not touch their hair while they are cheering. It's very distracting to see cheerleaders constantly pushing hair out of their face or off their shoulders when they are cheering. I recommend a standard that allows for individuality but also requires that the hair is anchored away from the face, using secure yet soft hair devices. If your squad performs stunts, they should secure the hair off the shoulders. I have seen more than one stunting cheerleader slide down the shoulder of a base person who had long hair that was not pulled back.

If your squad performs stunts, you will want to make sure that they do not wear bulky skirts that might be difficult to work in, or wear sweaters that are very loose (feet can get caught in loose-fitting sweaters). Check out your uniforms for safety, and make sure they are appropriate for your squad's style of cheering, for your school/community values, and for the weather.

As a safety precaution, if you have a squad member that is wearing a brace or cast, check it for hard or rough edges and cover or pad if necessary.

Definitions of Basic Terms

When you and your cheerleaders begin to add stunting skills to your performances, it is important that everyone understands basic terminology. Here is a list of the basic stunt terms used in cheerleading.

Aerial: An aerial stunt is performed in the air without contact.

Base Person: A base person has contact with the cheering surface and supports another person.

Basket Toss: A basket toss is a 3-4 person stunt where 2 people's hands are interlocked.

Bracer: A bracer has direct contact with a top person in a stunt but is not a base person. A bracer stabilizes a stunt.

Cradle Catch: A method for catching a top cheerleader. This is the way a top person is caught. The catchers have one arm under the back and the other under the thighs of the cheerleader being caught.

Drop: A person performing a drop is in an airborne position before landing on the performing surface, such as a knee drop, split drop, seat drop, or face-down drop. Do not allow your cheerleaders to perform these airborne drops because they can severely pull muscles and break bones.

Extended Stunt: An extended stunt is one where the base person's arms are extended above the head, holding weight.

Extension: An extension is a stunt where the top person is standing in the fully extended hands of the base person above the head. This stunt should always have a spotter!

Extension Prep: An extension prep is a stunt where the base persons' hands hold the feet of the top person at shoulder level (or near the collarbone area). This position precedes the extension.

Mount: A mount is made up of one or more base persons supporting one or more top persons.

Partner Stunt: A partner stunt is a mount that involves only two people.

Pendulum: A pendulum is a stunt that is performed at shoulder height or below and involves a top person who falls forward/backward and is caught by at least four people.

Pop: A pop is used to increase the height of the top person by the base persons' pushing motion or to release to a cradle catch.

Pyramid: A pyramid is made up of more than one mount.

Spotter: A spotter is a person who helps control a mount when building or dismounting. A spotter is in direct contact with the cheering surface and does not serve as a base person.

Stunt: A stunt is a mount, pyramid, or tumbling skill.

Suspended Roll: A suspended roll is a body rotation (head over heels) where the top person and the base person have continuous contact with hands and/or arms.

Suspended Splits: The suspended splits is a top person doing the splits between two bases who are holding the top person's hands continuously.

Sweep: A sweep occurs when the base persons release the top person to a cradle with a forward push.

Top Person: A top person in a mount or pyramid is the person being supported by the base persons.

Toss/Pitch: A toss or pitch occurs when the bases increase the height of the top person with a throwing motion. The top person loses contact with the base persons.

Totem Pole: A totem pole is a stunt that creates a low-to-high appearance when stunts are lined up one behind the other, such as a back thigh stand, a shoulder sit, and a shoulder stand.

Tumbling: Tumbling moves are rolls, inverted extended skills, and flips. Examples are a forward roll, a handstand, and a standing back tuck.

Twist: A twist occurs when the top person rotates perpendicular to the performing surface.

Two-High Mount: A two-high mount occurs when a top person, who is not in contact with the performing surface, is being supported by a base person who is in contact with the performing surface.

Mounts

As you work with your cheerleaders, you will want them to understand the basic skills needed to perform beginning mounts (one or more persons supported by one or more persons) before moving to pyramids (multiple mounts). Basic skills include correct base person and top person positions, how to safely step into basic mount positions, and how to progress from beginning to intermediate and advanced mounts. First, I will present important points that apply to the base person and top person (this is foundation information that you need to know before you begin). Then I will show you how to teach mounts by presenting seven mount progressions (how to go from one mount into another) that teach 15 different mount positions.

Focus Points

Before your cheerleaders begin to build mounts, you will need to make sure that everyone on the squad understands a few basic points. This foundation will hopefully create a mindset of serious safety during all stunting sessions.

1. Know what the mount looks like before you begin. Discuss the procedure with your cheerleaders before you start to build the mount, look at photos, and plan. Practice in steps.
2. Make sure your cheerleaders focus on what they are doing. No distractions, no goofing around, no laughing.
3. You can set the tone of mutual trust, confidence, and serious attitude by how you conduct the teaching sessions. Your cheerleaders need to learn that they can depend on each other when they are building mounts.
4. The spotter is the most important person during the learning sessions. It is imperative that you make sure that your cheerleaders are knowledgeable spotters. Everyone on your squad needs to practice spotting all of the mounts so that everyone understands the dynamics of each mount.
5. It is very important that your cheerleaders do not practice mounts without you, their coach. Make it very clear that they are not to practice mounts in their backyards or at any time that you are not present. You have an active role in every mount session.
6. The base person and the top person are to stay tight during the entire stunt. Discuss this before each new learning session and check to make sure that your cheerleaders are doing all of the basics correctly.
7. During the learning sessions, the spotters are actively involved in building the mounts. The base person and top person need to know where the spotters are standing for each mount. You will learn more about the mounts if you are also an active spotter for each mount as it is being learned.
8. The base person and top person are to keep contact until the top person is secure on the ground. Closely monitor all of the teaching sessions to make sure that your base persons and top persons are conscious of each others' safety.

Focus Points for the Base Person

Every person on the squad, whether they are a base person or not, should understand the following key points. Many cheerleaders serve as both base person and top person in different mounts, so everyone needs to understand the basics. Have your cheerleaders practice these positions before building a mount.

1. In a single lunge for an individual base person, make sure that the base person steps away from the bent leg. The bent leg should be at a right angle from the knee to the floor (see figure 8.1), and the knee should never extend beyond the foot (see figure 8.2). When teaching the single lunge to your squad, have them practice stepping away from the bent leg and check the angle.
2. Remind your cheerleaders that they should keep one foot slightly in front of the other to counteract imbalance.
3. In a single person double lunge, the knees should face outward, the back should be straight, the cheerleader should be in a slight squat position, and the hands should be above the knees (see figure 8.3). Your cheerleaders should never put pressure on their own knees or the knees of the top person. When teaching the double lunge,

check that the back is straight and that the hands form a "C" above each knee (the thumbs are facing each other on the inner thigh and the fingers are together on the outside of the thigh).

4. One type of double lunge is the flatback, which should be level enough so that a top person can balance on it when standing or kneeling (see figure 8.4). This flatback is taught later for the back stand mount (see pages 118-119).

Figure 8.1 Correct position of a single lunge for an individual base.

Figure 8.2 Incorrect position of a single lunge for an individual base.

Figure 8.3 Single person double lunge.

Figure 8.4 Flatback double lunge.

Focus Points for the Top Person

The top person needs to understand the sequence of the building procedure, but also needs to understand exactly what the base persons are doing at all times during the stunting process. Go through the sequence with the top person before starting to build a stunt, and make sure these key elements are understood.

1. When working with your cheerleaders, be sure to teach them that the top person needs to keep the body tight during the entire stunt—by controlling the head, hips, arms, legs, and torso—in

order to perform the stunt safely. Many times a stunt starts to fall because the top person has moved the head or hips, which throws off the balance of the stunt.

2. Watch that the top person climbs with a straight body and does not lean forward or backward. The top person should keep the head up and keep the center of gravity in the middle of the base level.
3. During the stunt progression, make sure that the top person locks the leg that steps on the base person before progressing to the next level or position. Have your cheerleaders practice the step-lock progression before stepping into a mount (see figure 8.5).
4. For the dismount, the top person should call "down" and take the responsibility for beginning the dismount. The top person should not panic, yell, or swing the arms. The top person is to stay tight and calm. The arms should be straight above the head or straight down at the sides to allow the spotters to assist.

Teaching Mounts

After you and your cheerleaders have discussed and practiced the focus points for the base person and top person positions, it's time to move into building mounts. The most important thing for you to remember when building mounts is to start with the basic positions—the beginning level—before progressing to the intermediate or advanced levels. Although there is a tendency for cheer-

Figure 8.5 Step-lock progression.

leaders to want to skip over the easier skills, keep them focused on mastering the beginning mounts before moving on to more challenging ones.

If your cheerleaders safely and successfully execute the beginning mounts, they will be ready for intermediate ones. I have provided seven mount progressions that teach 15 mounts. It's very important that these mounts are learned and practiced in the order they are presented here. As you follow the printed directions and the illustrations, learn the terms and the names at the same time. Do not advance to a new mount until you and your cheerleaders have mastered the one before it. As your cheerleaders learn these mounts, they are assembling the skills they'll need to build just about any pyramid because pyramids are made up of multiple mounts.

THIGH STAND

Figure 8.6a The thigh stand is a beginning stunt for two people that will help you teach your cheerleaders some of the basics about the step-lock approach to climbing. The base person steps into a single lunge.

Figure 8.6b The top person places one foot high on the base person's thigh, steps up, and locks the knee. The base person wraps an arm around the top person's upper thigh and holds the top person's foot with the other hand.

Figure 8.6c The base person's outside leg goes to a liberty position with the knee forward.

Figure 8.6d Another variation for the thigh stand position is the heel stretch.

Figure 8.6e To dismount, the top person brings the free leg to a liberty position with the knee forward.

Figure 8.6f The top person dismounts by stepping off the base person.

Spotting. As the stunt goes up, the spotter should stand behind the stunt with his or her hands on the waist of the top person. For the dismount, the spotter moves to the side of the stunt to assist the top person to the ground. After the thigh stand is mastered, a spotter is not required.

L STAND TO SHOULDER SIT

Figure 8.7a The L stand is a beginning stunt for two people that starts with a thigh stand. The base person steps into a single lunge.

Figure 8.7b The top person places one foot high on the base person's thigh, steps up, locks the knee . . .

Figure 8.7c . . . and immediately lifts the other leg into an L. The base person wraps an arm around the top person's upper thigh and reaches up to grab the top person's left leg. The base person should keep the arm locked and reach for the farthest point of the top person's calf.

Figure 8.7d To go into a shoulder sit from the L stand, the base person, while standing up, swings the top person's left leg around the shoulder.

Figure 8.7e The top person wraps her feet behind the base person's back and the base person wraps his hands around the top person's thighs with a firm grip.

Figure 8.7f To dismount, the base person reaches under the top person's thighs one hand at a time as the top person straightens the legs. The base person and the top person join hands.

Figure 8.7g The base person bends the knees and extends the arms to pop the top person to the ground; they hold hands until the top person is safely on the ground.

Spotting. The spotter stands to the side of the stunt, guiding the top person if needed. After the L stand and the shoulder sit are mastered, a spotter is not required.

BACK STAND TO SHOULDER STAND

Figure 8.8a The back stand is a beginning stunt for two people that starts with the base person in a double lunge with the hands above the knees.

Figure 8.8b The top person places one foot on the upper thigh of the base person and then steps up with other foot on the base's other thigh.

Figure 8.8c The top person then places one foot at a time on the lower back of the base person, straightening his or her legs to establish balance, and then slowly stands up.

Figure 8.8d To go into a shoulder stand from the back stand, the top person leans over to grasp the hands of the base person one hand at a time.

Figure 8.8e As the base person stands up, the top person places one foot on one of the base person's shoulders and then places the other foot on the other shoulder.

Figure 8.8f After the top person is secure on the base person's shoulders, the base person grabs the upper calves of the top person one at a time and holds them firmly.

Figure 8.8g To dismount, the top person reaches for the hands of the base person one at a time.

Figure 8.8h The base person locks the arms to give resistance as the top person steps off one leg at a time.

Figure 8.8i The top person lands on the balls of the feet and bends the knees. The base person leans slightly forward to help the top person to the ground.

Spotting. The spotter should stand to the side of the stunt, guiding or assisting with balance. After the back stand and the shoulder stand are mastered, a spotter is not required.

THIGH STAIR STEP TO DOUBLE BASE SHOULDER STAND

Figure 8.9a The thigh stair step is an intermediate stunt for three people. It begins with one base person in a single lunge and another base person standing close-by.

Figure 8.9b The top person (middle) places one foot on the upper thigh of the single lunge base person. The standing base person makes a stair step for the top person by placing a foot on the thigh of the single lunge base person.

Figure 8.9c The top person lifts her right foot to the thigh of the standing base person and shifts her weight to the stair step.

Figure 8.9d The standing base person wraps an arm around the upper thigh of the top person, who places his or her left foot on the shoulder of the single lunge base person. The weight of the top person is on the standing base person.

Figure 8.9e To go into a double base shoulder stand from the thigh stair step, the top person grabs the outside hands of both bases.

Figure 8.9f Then the top person shifts weight to the leg that is on the shoulder of the single lunge base person, who stands up as the standing base person drops his lifted foot. The top person steps to the shoulder of the second standing base person.

(continued)

THIGH STAIR STEP TO DOUBLE BASE SHOULDER STAND *(continued)*

Figure 8.9g After the top person is secure, the top person stands up as each base person grabs an upper calf and a foot of the top person.

Figure 8.9h Once the top person is stabilized, the bases may remove their outside hands from the top person's foot and do an outside high V.

Figure 8.9i To dismount from a double base shoulder stand, the top person reaches down one hand at a time to grab the outside hands of the bases.

Figure 8.9j The top person steps off one foot at a time as the bases guide the top person down and lock their arms to give resistance.

Figure 8.9k The bases lean slightly forward to help the top person to the ground. The top person lands on the balls of the feet and bends the knees while still holding onto the bases' hands.

Spotting. The spotter should stand behind the stunt to help guide or stabilize. After the thigh stair step and the double base shoulder stand are mastered, a spotter is not required.

RUSSIAN LIFT TO TRIPLE BASE STRADDLE

Figure 8.10a The Russian lift is a stunt for two people. It is a beginning/intermediate stunt because the base person has the arms extended and is holding weight, but the top person's legs are not above the base person's head. However, this stunt is not difficult. Begin the Russian lift by first starting with a back thigh stand. The base person steps into a double lunge and the top person steps onto the upper thighs of the base person one foot at a time.

Figure 8.10b From the back thigh stand position, the top person bends at the knees and places the arms in a T position while the base person grabs under the arms.

Figure 8.10c As the base person bends at the knees and gives a strong pop with the arms and the legs, the top person lifts the legs, grabs the calf/ankle area, and locks out the arms.

Figure 8.10d The triple base straddle lift is an advanced stunt because the arms of all the bases are extended and holding weight; the top person's body is above the base persons' heads. To go into the triple base straddle lift from a Russian lift, two additional bases come behind the Russian lift and each base person grabs an upper thigh and an ankle of the top person.

Figure 8.10e The Russian lift base person bends the knees and the leg base persons extend the top person as the Russian lift base person moves the hands to the top person's seat.

Figure 8.10f To dismount, the outside bases walk their legs together . . .

Figure 8.10g . . . and all three bases gently lower the top person's feet to the ground.

Spotting. The spotter should stand behind both stunts to help guide or stabilize. After the Russian lift and the triple base straddle are mastered, a spotter is not required.

SHOULDER SIT TO EXTENSION PREP TO DOUBLE BASE EXTENSION TO CRADLE

Figure 8.11a The shoulder sit is an intermediate stunt for two people. The base person steps into a single lunge with her arms behind her.

Figure 8.11b The top person, standing behind the lunge, steps high on the thigh of the base person, locks the leg, and wraps the opposite leg around the base person's shoulder.

Figure 8.11c The top person sits as the base person stands up.

Figure 8.11d The extension prep is an intermediate stunt for four people. To go into an extension prep from the shoulder sit, the top person unwraps the feet from the base person's back and lets them dangle in front of the base person.

Figure 8.11e Two additional bases come from the sides and face each other and each one then grasps the top person's feet at toe and heel areas. As the shoulder sit base bends down . . .

Figure 8.11f . . . the top person stands up into the hands of the two new bases.

(continued)

SHOULDER SIT TO EXTENSION PREP TO DOUBLE BASE EXTENSION TO CRADLE *(continued)*

Figure 8.11g The shoulder sit base stays behind the extension prep, which is now ready to extend.

Figure 8.11i The cradle is an advanced stunt for three people and requires a spotter. To cradle the top person from the extension prep position, the bases bend their knees, pop the top person upward a little, and move their arms to catch the top person's back and thighs.

Figure 8.11h A double base extension is an advanced stunt for three people and requires a spotter. To move into the double base extension from the extension prep position, the two bases, on a count of 1-2, bend their knees and then stand while extending their arms over their heads. The shoulder sit base remains behind and acts as a spotter. The top person is completely tight and does not move. To dismount, the bases bring the top person back down to the extension prep position shown in figure 8.11g.

Figure 8.11j The spotter moves in to scoop the head and the shoulders of the top person by placing the arms under the top person's arm pits and cradling the head and the shoulder area.

Figure 8.11k During the cradle, the top person lifts the arms to touchdown position, brings the legs together after the pop, and bends at the waist for the cradle. After the bases and spotter move in to position and as the top person is in the air, the top person's arms go into a T position.

Figure 8.11l From the cradle, the bases set out the top person feetfirst.

Spotting. For the shoulder sit, the spotter stands to the side. For the extension prep, the spotter moves to the front since the shoulder sit base is already in the back. After they are mastered, the shoulder sit and the extension prep do not require a spotter. For the double base extension and the cradle, a second spotter stands to the side of the required spotter during the learning process. A double base extension and a cradle always require at least one spotter, even after they are mastered.

SHOULDER STAND TO TRIPLE BASE EXTENDED SPLITS

Figure 8.12a The shoulder stand is an intermediate stunt for two people. The base person steps into a lunge and places the arms above the head to grab the hands of the top person, who is standing behind. The top person grabs the hands of the base person and then steps one foot onto the base person's upper thigh.

Figure 8.12b As the top person steps onto the base person's shoulder, the base person keeps the arms above the head and gives resistance to the top person.

Figure 8.12c After the top person has both feet on the shoulders of the base person, the top person should lock the legs. The top person keeps contact with the hands of the base person. The base person stands up after the top person has stepped onto the base person's shoulders and has locked the legs.

Figure 8.12d After the stunt is steady, the top person stands up and the base person grabs the top person's upper calves.

Figure 8.12e The triple base extended splits is an advanced stunt for four people. To go into the triple base extended splits from the shoulder stand, two additional bases move in from the sides and stand beside the shoulder stand. The shoulder stand base becomes a post, which means that the top person grabs the base person's hands for support.

Figure 8.12f The two new bases move in to grab the upper thighs and the ankles of the top person. On a count of 1-2, all three bases bend their knees and then pop the top person into the extended splits.

Figure 8.12g To dismount, the three bases lower the top person to shoulder level and the top person grabs the shoulders of the post person.

Figure 8.12h The side bases bring the top person's legs down and the top person lands on the feet.

Spotting. The spotter should stand behind both stunts. After the shoulder stand and the triple base extended splits are mastered, a spotter is not required.

Pyramids

A pyramid is made up of multiple mounts (see figure 8.13). For instance, a pyramid could have a shoulder stand in the middle and two shoulder sits on the sides. Any pyramid can be broken down into at least two component mounts. Be sure to work with your cheerleaders on the separate components before putting everything together as a pyramid. If your cheerleaders have been able to master these seven mount progressions, then they should be able to build almost any pyramid. Before you allow your cheerleaders to try intermediate mounts (usually shoulder level), they should master the beginning mounts (usually thigh or waist level), and before they try advanced mounts—which usually involve a toss, an extension, or a transition of some difficulty—they should be able to skillfully execute beginning and intermediate mounts. Stay firm and committed to basic mounts before allowing your cheerleaders to try the advanced pyramids.

Besides learning new mounts and pyramids at summer camp or at clinics, you may also be interested in learning new mounts by using my *Partner Stunts and Pyramids* book and my mounts and pyramids videos, which are available from *Cheer In Style*, P.O. Box 207, Lee's Summit, MO 64063. Toll free number: 800-862-4337.

Figure 8.13 Examples of pyramids.

Summary

Here are the key points about safety and stunts outlined in this chapter.

- Since cheerleaders train as athletes, they need specific safety guidelines.
- The National Federation of State High School Associations makes

their *High School Spirit Rules Book* and safety videos available each year.

- As the coach, your responsibility is to locate, learn, teach, implement, and monitor the safety guidelines for your squad(s).
- There are general safety guidelines for all coaches that establish a safety foundation for any type of cheerleading.
- The spotter is the guardian of safety because the spotter must be in a position to prevent injuries with special emphasis on protecting the head, neck, and back areas.
- Spotters must be able to quickly counteract movements of the top person and be prepared to respond to possible emergencies.
- Cheerleaders need to know and understand personal appearance guidelines for cheerleading, such as not wearing jewelry, wearing safe hair devices, and having short fingernails.
- Coaches need to understand the definitions of basic cheerleading terms in order to properly coach mounts and pyramids.
- When learning basic mounts, the base person and the top person need to focus, understand the stunt procedure, and stay tight during the entire stunt.
- Beginning mounts are those stunts involving two people where the top person is standing no higher than the base person's thigh or waist.
- Intermediate mounts are those mounts performed at shoulder level.
- Advanced mounts and pyramids usually involve a toss, an extension, or a more difficult transition.
- A pyramid progression involves mastering beginning and intermediate mounts and pyramids before moving up to advanced mounts and pyramids.

Part IV

Coaching Cheerleading Events

Chapter 9

© Thomas J. Benincas, Jr.

Cheering at Athletic Events

Everything you do prepares your cheerleaders for "The Big Game." The effectiveness of your cheerleading program will hinge on the effectiveness of your cheerleaders during an athletic event. How well your squad can generate spirit, lead a crowd, promote sportsmanship, or work with other spirit groups will determine if your program is successful or not. It's your responsibility to make sure your cheerleaders have the opportunities as well as the skills to provide leadership during athletic events.

Your cheerleaders play a pivotal role during athletic events because they not only lead the crowd, they also control the crowd, represent the school to visitors, and sometimes work with a mascot or other spirit groups. In this chapter I will present ideas for fostering crowd involvement and crowd control, suggestions on how to develop a program that emphasizes the importance of leading through good sportsmanship, and tips on creating a Pep Club or Spirit Club in your school. Be sure to get prior approval from the school administration for all crowd involvement ideas.

Communicating With the Crowd

Communicating with the crowd means leading the crowd. Your cheerleaders serve as the leadership link between the fans and the team. The goal of crowd communication is to involve the crowd in the cheers and chants with the purpose of inspiring the team to victory. Your cheerleaders are meeting this goal if the crowd responds to and supports the squad's efforts—no easy task.

One of my favorite techniques for building crowd control leadership is to conduct "situational cheering" activities during practice. I call out game situations for the particular sport, and the cheerleaders respond with the appropriate actions. Some of the situations call for specific types of chants (such as offense or defense) and some call for specific action (such as in response to rowdy fans). We spend time discussing how to handle the game action situations and how to respond. In order to communicate with and inspire the crowd, your cheerleaders must be able to recognize the game situation and lead the appropriate cheer or chant that will fire-up the team. Simulating the cheering situation will help your squad practice how to quickly respond and will help them become more effective, informed leaders.

Following are a variety of crowd involvement ideas to help promote participation. Remember that sometimes a new idea will catch on and become an instant success, and sometimes it fizzles. Just make sure your cheerleaders continue to try new ideas in their ongoing efforts to unify and lead the crowd in support of athletic events. During the game, leadership has the starring role and entertainment has a minor role. Keep your cheerleaders on track.

CROWD INVOLVEMENT IDEAS

1. Class Spirit Cans. Arrange for each class to have a brightly colored plastic trash can with the class name and graduation year on it (either painted or vinyl letters). These spirit cans can be used for class competitions and relays during pep rallies, and to get the class to yell together during games. The inside of the lid should have something on it to provoke a response: the graduation year, one of the school colors, or a word to shout, such as "Go." A representative from each class could help the cheerleaders when these spirit cans are utilized during the game.

2. Over-Sized Letters. Cut out foamboard or plywood letters that you can use to feature the school initials, mascot name, or motivational words like "Go, Fight, Win," or the school colors.

3. Class Spirit Sticks. A spirit stick is a painted dowel rod or plastic tubing that is used to get everyone to yell. They are usually about 12-15 inches long and easy to see. Each class can have its own spirit stick that a class representative waves in the air to get the class to yell during pep rallies or games.

4. Over-Sized Spirit Stick. This is a huge spirit stick made out of a carpet roll (the thick tubing used inside a roll of carpet) that can be painted in school colors. Because of its high visibility, the giant spirit stick can get the crowd yelling during the game. It can also be used for class competitions or specific word responses.

5. Warm-Up Basketball. Paint the warm-up basketball in your school colors. When it is bounced during the warm-up, everyone yells "Go," your school name, or your mascot. Some schools make this a tradition before all basketball games.

6. Spirit Bell. Paint a large bell in your school colors. When the bell is sounded, there is a certain word or crowd response. The class that yells the loudest gets their graduation year painted on the bell.

7. Tigers Rule. Make a huge yardstick with a slogan on it to use as a spirit stick. Other slogans to choose from:

- By the yard it's hard, by the inch it's a cinch.
- Add up a victory.
- Our spirit is immeasurable.
- Spirit is the measure of our success.

8. Tigers Are Cookin'. Put letters on aprons to lead the crowd.

9. Giant Helmets. Make giant football helmets out of posterboard and use them to lead chants or do spell-outs.

10. Cheer Box. Make a giant replica of the Cheer detergent box and use it to get the crowd to yell during pep rallies and games.

11. Pompon Spell-Outs. Squad members arrange themselves in a tight group of low-medium-high placement to form pompon letters for the school initials, the mascot, school colors, or motivational words. In this position, they can lead spell-outs during cheers or anytime during the game.

12. Spirit Ladder. Label the rungs of a ladder from top to bottom with words like "Dull, Climbing, Excited, Fire-Up, Psyched,

Rowdy, Red Hot." The louder the fans yell, the higher the mascot, teacher, player, or cheerleader climbs.

13. Hat Day. The tops of hats have letters that are used to spell out words during the pep rally or the game.

14. Shower the Tigers With a Victory. Sew large letters into umbrellas. When the umbrella is popped open, everyone yells.

15. Nature's Spirit Stick. Use a branch to lead chants and class competitions to represent that your team will get a Vic-Tree.

16. Giant Stuffed Mascot. Use a giant stuffed mascot with a slogan on the back to lead chants at pep rallies and games.

17. Big News. Put crowd involvement words on large pieces of newspaper.

18. Inspirational Signs. When each player is introduced, have people in the crowd hold up signs that say TOUGH, DYNAMITE, SUPER, GREAT, TERRIFIC, FANTASTIC, SENSATIONAL, WOW, WAY TO GO.

19. Building Spirit. Make giant replicas of a hammer (hammer out a victory), a saw (I never saw such a team), pliers (comply with the coach's plan), and a wrench (it will be a wrenching game), and lead the crowd with chants.

20. Helium Balloons. Fill large balloons with helium and hand them out at the football game. Everyone lets them go at kickoff or the first touchdown.

21. Music. Select a certain song or part of a song that the crowd can do a special clap with and yell certain words with. The music serves as a cue to get the crowd to participate.

22. Hula Hoop Signs. Cover hula hoops with banner paper and draw your mascot face or put words/letters on them to lead the crowd.

23. Giant Hands. Make large hands out of neon posterboard and glue to paint sticks. These can be used to lead the crowd to sway, wave, clap, or alternate arms raising up and down.

24. Paper-Covered Boxes. Cover boxes with banner paper and write the words the crowd should yell on each side of the box. The box can be turned to the appropriate word to get the crowd to yell.

25. Cheer-O-Meter. People hold signs ranging from HO HUM to SUPER FANTASTIC SPIRIT. A runner with a huge arrow races back and forth to register the volume of the noise. This can be used during a game, a pep rally, or a class competition.

26. Mascot Faces. Make mascot "masks" with posterboard and write a huge GO on the back. These can be glued onto paint sticks (from hardware stores) and can be used effectively during games or pep rallies. The cheerleaders lead the chant "Go . . . (mascot name)," with the fans turning the masks back and forth.

27. Posterboard Squares. Cut out large squares of your school colors, gluing one color to the other so they can be flipped back and forth. These can be used for school color chants.

28. Floor Spell-Outs. Representatives from each class use their bodies to spell out words to yell during pep rallies.

29. Giant Flag. Cheerleaders, class representatives, players, or teachers run with a giant school flag around the court or the track before or during games. The giant flag can also be driven around the track on a decorated golf cart, on a horse, or on a minibike.

30. Thermometer Spirit Stick. Make a large replica of a real thermometer and write SPIRIT FEVER or (MASCOT) HOT SPIRIT on the side of it. Use it to lead "fire-up" chants.

HANDS ACROSS THE STADIUM

I had been asked to organize 200 cheerleaders who were going to perform at the Hula Bowl game in Hawaii. Of course I said yes! I decided to try using the giant neon hands as a prop for both the stands and for the pregame routine on the field. Each cheerleader received two orange neon hands cut out of posterboard and glued to paint sticks (the hands are about 12 inches in size). During our training session, I taught them a routine using the hands as props and also worked on motions that could be used in the stands. Our goal was to create a dramatic impact in the huge stadium. The four hundred waving neon hands were so popular with the people attending the game that some of them were stolen from us after our performance. We had no trouble finding them though: We could easily spot lone orange hands waving from across the field.

Crowd Control

Crowd involvement and crowd control are very similar in that they both involve cheerleaders leading the crowd. Crowd control differs from crowd involvement, though, in that the control centers around directing or diverting the crowd's behavior, usually during undesirable responses to the game (such as booing). It is the responsibility of the cheerleading squad to know how to handle these inappropriate behaviors during a game.

Unsportsmanlike conduct during athletic events is usually caused by a small percentage of alumni students, parents, or members of the student body. The inappropriate behavior generally occurs following a call by the referee or isolated incidents during the game itself. Booing, whistling, use of foul language, or throwing items are the common responses. Even though your school should already have a sportsmanship policy regarding these behaviors, there are some things that your cheerleaders can do to control the crowd in a positive way. At the first sign of undesirable behavior, they should start an easy chant that everyone knows and will yell with (or a traditional favorite) to divert attention away from the negative behavior.

There might be times when sections of the crowd will become too rowdy for the cheerleaders to control. Inform school officials to take appropriate action during these incidents. Often, the strength, courage, and effectiveness of the school administration will be an important factor in the recurrence or the severity of these incidents. Cheerleaders need to do their part to control the crowd in a positive manner, but the ultimate responsibility for controlling undesirable behavior rests with the school administration.

Here are some specific crowd control ideas that might work for you, depending on the circumstances:

- Have your mascot go up into the crowd and help the cheerleaders lead a popular chant that everyone knows and will yell with.
- Ask your band to start the school song, a favorite song for your school, or a special beat to get everyone involved in clapping.
- Start a crowd involvement cheer that everyone knows.
- Use signs to get the crowd to yell.
- Start a class competition chant using graduation years.

If crowd control is a problem at your school, set up a meeting with administrators, sport team coaches, Student Council officers, and the Booster Club to discuss the issue. I have heard about schools that encountered volatile game situations involving fans and chose to have the referees clear the gym of all spectators. In another incident, because of some potentially dangerous circumstances, all of the games held at a specific school were played without spectators. Consult with your high school activities association or the National Federation of State High School Associations if you need further crowd control measures.

Leading Through Good Sportsmanship

Remind your cheerleaders to always cheer *for* your team and *never against* the opposing team. Negative cheering is poor sportsmanship. Do not allow your cheerleaders to exhibit disrespectful behavior in any way. Your cheerleading squad must exemplify the highest of good sportsmanship standards.

One of the most important ways your cheerleaders can get others to follow them during a game is to gain the respect of the school and community. Since the cheerleaders are serving in an important leadership position, they need to remember that they will ultimately lead through example.

Basic Cheer Guidelines

During a game or pep rally, the purpose of cheerleaders is to lead the crowd and to control the crowd's response. The words of the cheers and chants need to reflect the game action and should not have suggestive or inflammatory words. In order to be understood and followed easily, cheerleaders should emphasize each word, look at the crowd when cheering, and display enthusiastic facial expression. If a crowd starts booing, cheerleaders should divert the crowd's attention by starting a popular chant or cheer. Do not use bells, horns, or noisemakers.

Appropriate Times To Cheer

The most appropriate times for cheerleaders to cheer are when the team comes onto the floor or field, drives for a score, or defends the goal. Other cheering opportunities occur when one of your players or an opponent leaves the game after playing spectacularly. You may also cheer when a substitution is made or as a tribute to an injured player on your team.

Inappropriate Times to Cheer

Do not cheer when an opposing player is injured; when an opponent makes a mistake; when the opposing team is being penalized; during a free throw, a serve, or a dive; when the quarterback is calling signals; or during announcements made over the public address system.

Opportune Times to Perform

Gear your time-out performances for the specific sport, cheering surface, and time allotment. Meet with sport team coaches to verify the amount of time available for cheering: for instance, in basketball, time outs are only 60 seconds long. Cheerleaders should wait until the players are off the floor before they go out and should get off the floor 5-10 seconds before the time out is over. Remember that your performances are limited to pregame, between quarters, during noninjury time outs, halftime, and postgame.

Communicating With Visiting Cheerleaders

Your cheerleaders serve as student ambassadors for visiting cheerleaders. Ways to promote good relations between squads include sending a letter to (or calling) the visiting squad to welcome them to your school; sending a map to indicate what door to use, where to go once they arrive, and where to find restroom facilities; or setting up a hospitality room that provides snacks and a place to leave personal items.

Before the game starts, greet the visiting squad and mutually decide how you will take turns cheering during the game and whether you will trade sides for a welcome cheer. Also, convey any particular information they should know about your facilities (such as where or where not to cheer). If possible, meet the coach of the visiting cheerleaders and answer any questions. Touch base with them at halftime to make sure everything is going well and offer to provide them beverages. Tell them good-bye when they leave and walk them to their cars or buses if necessary.

Safety and Supervision

To ensure the safety of your cheerleaders, you (or a qualified assistant) need to be at every event where they are involved (home and away). Evaluate the cheering area for safety, make sure that your cheerleaders follow all safety rules, and watch for potential hazards. Ideally, each school provides a bus for the cheerleaders to ride for away events: Cheerleaders should not be driving on their own.

There have been a few occasions when the physical safety of a cheerleading squad was in jeopardy (such as a volatile crowd situation or a parking lot disturbance). Cheerleaders' parents who attend games can also help monitor situations that may arise. It is important to be aware of potential dangers and take necessary precautions (such as making sure your cheerleaders always walk together as a group). Even though it would be rare that your cheerleaders may be endangered in any way, decide in advance what your procedure will be in case of emergency; know who to contact, where to meet, and how to respond.

Combining Resources

In order to build spirit in the school, your cheerleaders will need to work with and help coordinate the efforts of the Spirit Club or Pep Club, the school mascot, and other groups such as a dance or drill team or student government committees. The more your cheerleaders can involve students from other areas, the more support will be generated for athletics and for the school. Keep the lines of communication open with all of these student groups in order to effectively combine the resources from each other.

Pep Club

The purpose of a Pep Club is to provide the opportunity for students to sit together during a game to support the team by cheering with the cheerleaders. Your role as coach would require that you help your cheerleaders learn how to work with the Pep Club, since supporting athletic events is the number one role for both groups.

Pep Clubs used to be very popular, but over time many of their traditions died out. Schools that are already effective in getting students to support athletic events may not need a Pep Club tradition. In general, Pep Clubs have gone from being very structured to very informal, from uniforms to jeans and T-shirts. Formerly, they used to provide the framework from which cheerleaders emerged (meaning that you had to serve in Pep Club before you tried out), but that is no longer the case at most schools.

I have always favored the idea of a Pep Club (which I prefer to call a Spirit Club) that involves many students in supporting athletic events. I also favor the requirement of Spirit Club service that precedes cheerleading tryouts. It makes sense to me that the leaders need to emerge from the support group that backs them up when they cheer. At the very core of the cheerleader's responsibility is a commitment to serve the school. The sincerity of this commitment is exemplified by Spirit Club service.

The Spirit Club idea that I like the most I found at a school where all athletes were members of the Spirit Club. When they were not competing in their sport, they were expected to support the other athletes in theirs. The quality of the school spirit, sportsmanship, and commitment were outstanding.

Starting a Pep Club

If your school is considering starting a Pep Club, you may want to get involved at the onset since it could directly benefit your cheerleading program. A Pep Club opens up opportunities for increased student involvement and greater school spirit and provides a solid core of involved fans who will yell with the cheers and chants. This verbal support will hopefully spread to other fans as well. The atmosphere of louder fans and solid support during a game can unify the forces of school spirit and electrify the team.

When I helped establish a Spirit Club at one school, the first thing we did was ask the teachers to give us lists of the most popular and involved students in the school. We printed up invitations for these student leaders to attend the foundation meeting of the Spirit Club to get it off the ground. We also offered a few other incentives—entertainment and food—to get them to come, and it worked. This core of students made a commitment to improve the school spirit and initiate the first Spirit Club at the school. From that beginning, other students joined. The organization had a good reputation before it even got off the ground because it was organized by popular students who wanted to make a difference.

Some schools get their Spirit Clubs going through their Student Council. Some are started by friends of the cheerleaders and the team members. Others are formed by enlisting a drill or dance team as the core of the group. Some high schools allow their middle or junior high students to join the club as well.

STARTING A SPIRIT CLUB IN YOUR SCHOOL

If you are thinking about establishing a Spirit Club for your school, here are some ideas that will help you get organized:

1. **Conduct a Spirit Questionnaire** at the beginning of the year to find out the spirit issues at your school. Include a sign-up form for the Spirit Club to assess interest.
2. **During registration,** have a booth set up and information available about the proposed Spirit Club. Make a presentation during registration or orientation.
3. **Make Spirit Club membership** a prerequisite for cheerleading tryouts.
4. **Set up an organizational meeting** and get volunteers to give suggestions on how to get students to join. Plan a party to get things rolling.
5. **Locate interested faculty** or administration members who would be willing to provide adult leadership.
6. **Start thinking of possible names** for the club, for instance, Panther Pack, Rowdy Raiders, Bleacher Creatures.

In order to get students to want to join your Spirit Club, remember that everyone wants to feel important. You need to be able to offer traditions, special events, recognition, and fun. For instance, I know some schools that have a special dance and cookout every year. Spirit

Club members should have a special place to sit, get to line up on the field for team introductions, ride buses to the games, get into the game for free, and have matching T-shirts to wear on game days. Membership in the school's Spirit Club needs to be exciting in order to be successful.

Your cheerleaders will need to understand that they are an extension of the Spirit Club (and an extension of the whole school for that matter). Cheerleaders and Spirit Club members should have meetings together occasionally in order to be organized for the games. This will provide an excellent opportunity for the cheerleaders to teach new cheers and chants, and for both organizations to discuss some new crowd involvement ideas and plan how to promote good sportsmanship. Your role as the coach is to help keep communication smooth and the meetings organized. You also need to make sure that the Pep Club or Spirit Club members support the cheerleaders and do not work against them. It's important that a smooth relationship exists between the cheerleaders and the Spirit Club members in order to boost school spirit and team morale.

Some schools have wonderful student support without an organized Spirit Club. The quality of the involvement and the commitment to the support of the athletic programs is the key to success: A Spirit Club as such does not guarantee good school spirit. As the coach, you and your cheerleaders will need to try some ideas to see what works in your school. Since you already have your hands full with the cheerleaders, you will need to find other adults to help sponsor the proposed Spirit Club (or merely help you handle whatever student support you receive at the games). You should not have to coach the cheerleaders and sponsor the Spirit Club.

Working With Other Groups

Besides the Spirit Club, the other two groups your cheerleaders may work with are the student government organization and the drill or dance team at your school. In some schools, drill or dance team members sit together at the games and support the cheerleaders during cheers and chants. Some schools combine the cheerleaders and the drill or dance team members into a large Spirit Squad, whose members support each other throughout the year, even performing together for special events. You should build a relationship with the drill or dance program because the unity of the two programs will provide a solid foundation for effective student support and school spirit.

In most schools, the student government representatives are also students who play sports, serve on the drill or dance team, cheer, play in the band, and belong to other organizations within the school. Good support from the student government will also help establish support for your cheerleading program and boost student involvement. Student government members can help your cheerleaders reinforce good sportsmanship during athletic events by serving as good role models, showing courtesy to visitors, and demonstrating positive cheering support.

Working With Mascots

Mascots can help build spirit, pride, and sportsmanship at your school by serving as positive role models and sources of inspiration during the game. Your mascot can greatly enhance the effectiveness of your cheerleading squad while boosting school spirit. Some mascots wear a full body costume. When the person inside is hidden, the mascot can more easily display a personality that represents the spirit of the school.

Courtesy of Heritage High School

Some mascots who wear a costume that does not cover the face actually do the cheers with the cheerleaders as another squad member. Mascots in full costume should not be involved in stunts or spotting. A mascot that cheers or one that doesn't have the face covered, however, has a harder time developing a "mascot personality." But both types of mascots can be extremely effective in helping the cheerleaders with exciting crowd involvement ideas. They can boost pride in the school by how they present the mascot persona, how they work with the cheerleading squad, and how they exemplify good sportsmanship. They can also serve as school spirit ambassadors by giving candy to children, going up into the stands to shake hands with fans, or holding up signs to get people to yell.

MASCOT TRYOUTS

I was so excited to be asked to judge mascot tryouts at Central Missouri State University in Warrensburg, Missouri. The Mule mascot at CMSU was popular, and there were many candidates to choose from. Since the university did not have a judging form for mascot tryouts, I was asked to bring my own. I decided to focus on a few key areas for the judging form: personality projection, crowd leadership, and expression of emotion. To judge personality projection, the candidate performed a short skit. For crowd leadership, the candidate used signs, a megaphone, or other props to get the crowd to yell. To judge expression of emotion, the candidate was given an actual game situation and then was to respond with the emotion that would be conveyed to the crowd. The mascot that was chosen became an important part of the visual representation of CMSU spirit.

You will need to have meetings with the mascot to plan entertainment and involvement ideas for the games or pep rallies. Try to get the mascot involved in all school spirit activities and include the mascot in some of your cheers and chants by holding signs or leading the crowd with a megaphone. Your mascot should develop a separate personality and display an identity and an independence during the games. If possible, develop some unique traditions centered around the mascot, such as where the mascot stands during player introductions, what the mascot might do with the band, or a traditional cheer with the mascot featured.

Summary

Here are the key points to consider when you are planning for athletic events:

- Leading the crowd is one of the most important responsibilities your cheerleaders face.
- Always cheer for your team and never against the opposing team.
- The purpose of a crowd involvement idea is to get the crowd to do the same thing at the same time to support the team.
- Crowd involvement ideas include waving a spirit stick, using a spirit bell, pompon spell-outs, music, giant hands, a cheer-o-meter, floor spell-outs, or a giant flag.
- Crowd control centers around directing or diverting the crowd's behavior, usually during undesirable responses to the game (such as booing).
- The cheerleading squad must know how to handle inappropriate behavior by the crowd during a game.
- Your mascot and/or your band can help you during crowd control challenges.
- Cheerleaders should always lead through example, upholding the highest principles of good sportsmanship at all times.
- Know when cheerleaders should cheer and when they should not cheer.
- The cheerleaders from your school serve as student ambassadors for visiting cheerleaders.

- Promote good relations with a visiting squad by doing things like setting up a hospitality room for them, deciding in advance about taking turns cheering on the floor during the game, and discussing the welcome cheer exchange between sides.
- To ensure the safety of your cheerleaders, the coach (or a qualified assistant) needs to be at every event (both home and away).
- A Pep Club, or Spirit Club, can greatly enhance your quest for spirited student involvement during games.
- When establishing a Spirit Club, remember that everyone wants to feel important.
- It is possible to have good school spirit without an organized Pep Club or Spirit Club.
- Your mascot can greatly enhance the effectiveness of your cheerleading squad and also boost school spirit.

Chapter 10

Courtesy of Oakwood High School

Building School Spirit

Thousands of schools conduct pep rallies before football and basketball games during the school year. These pep rallies are usually organized by the cheerleaders and student government representatives. You will need to understand everything that goes into these pep rallies so that you can serve as an effective leader during the planning and implementing process. Pep rallies can make a dramatic impact on school spirit and student support. They are not only fun, they get everyone riled up for the game!

In this chapter I will discuss how to organize the pep rally and also share some great pep rally ideas. Since building school spirit is one of the key responsibilities of your cheerleaders, I will also present many ongoing ideas for developing and maintaining the excitement of raising school spirit.

Planning the Pep Rally

Organization and communication are the cornerstones of pep rally success. What may appear on the surface to be a high energy spontaneous havin'-a-good-time pep rally in actuality requires hours of planning and much behind-the-scenes support. It involves working with the Pep Club, student government, other school organizations, school administrators, faculty, and student body.

If you are a new coach, you will need to learn the specific steps to take to organize, obtain approval for, and promote your pep rally. If the pep rally dates have not been scheduled before the season begins, check with sport coaches or administrators at least two weeks ahead of when you want to have the event so that you can mutually establish the date for the pep rally. Meet with your cheerleaders to discuss the pep rally, sharing any specific information about the upcoming rivals and ideas on how to get the team, the students, and the community pumped up for the game. Together, try to think up some motivational slogans that might be used in a skit, a chant, or a class competition.

FIRE-UP YOUR SPIRIT

This was to be the extravaganza pep rally of all time, and we worked hard preparing for it. We decorated the stage area in our gym to look like the side of a fire truck (we painted large cardboard sheets and then assembled them in front of the stage so that when you were standing on the stage, it looked like you were standing on a fire truck). We borrowed a siren and a flashing red light to complete the scene. At the beginning of the pep rally, the cheerleaders all came out on to the stage with fire hats on, leading "Fire-Up With Spirit" chants. We used the siren and flashing light during some of our chants, and borrowed a firefighter's coat and hat for the coach to wear (who talked about "burning up the field" at the game that night). Our spirit was red hot for that special pep rally!

Components of the Pep Rally

Most pep rallies have the same basic components, with many variations possible and welcome. Review the following components of a typical pep rally and decide which ones might be used for yours.

- **The Pep Band.** Make arrangements with the band director in advance to schedule the Pep Band to be part of the activities. Fast-paced music really gets everyone excited at the beginning of the pep rally as people enter the gym.
- **Spirit Chants.** The cheerleaders should explode onto the floor, leading chants that are short, popular, and familiar.
- **Pep Talk.** Fire-up the crowd with a pep talk delivered by the head cheerleader, the coach, the captain of the team, the student body president, or anyone else that would be effective in getting the pep rally off to a spirited start. The pep talk should include a brief welcome and reference to the upcoming game.
- **Cheer.** The cheer should be a favorite one of the entire school, with the costumed mascot helping to get everyone to yell with the cheerleaders.
- **Introduction of the Coach and a Brief Talk About the Game.** The coach can also introduce the team captains, who may or may not say a few words about the upcoming game.
- **Good Luck or Sportsmanship Cheer.** This cheer will be more effective if it has a pyramid, a unique ending, or ends with a crowd response to unify the entire school in anticipation of a victory.
- **Short Skit.** The skit should be fun and center on the mascot, game, spirit in general, or personalities within the school. It should star students and teachers who can really make a skit work. The punch line at the end of the skit should tie everything together. A good way to end is with a pun or short spirit chant.
- **Class Competition Chants and Contests.** Whether a chant or a contest, make sure that the ending features a show of unity for the entire school.
- **Fight Song or School Song.** This is always an effective way to unify the crowd in pride and spirit and using a Pep Band really makes a difference.
- **Dance Performance.** A high-energy dance routine, performed by your drill or dance team (if you have one) or by your cheerleaders, is also a good addition to the pep rally.

Components can be expanded, eliminated, or combined. Stay focused on the primary purposes of having a pep rally: to raise school spirit, honor athletes, and celebrate the pride and the tradition at your school.

Working With the Pep Club and Other Organizations

Before the actual pep rally day, you and your cheerleaders should meet with the Pep Club. Discuss their involvement, invite their ideas, and make sure they know the schedule of events. The Pep Club should sit in the same section together during the pep rally and serve as the primary catalyst for the other students. The cheerleaders need to work with the Pep Club or Spirit Club members in advance to make sure that they know everything that will happen at the pep rally. In some schools, it's the Pep Club that puts on the skit. Members are also involved in the class competition chant or contest. Make sure that the Pep Club has a primary role in the pep rally.

Make arrangements with the band director to get everything organized for the pep rally. If the band is going to be involved, make sure the director receives a copy of the exact pep rally schedule. If the cheerleaders are performing a routine to the fight song, both groups should practice together. If the dance or drill team will be performing with the band during the pep rally, these groups need to rehearse in advance.

If you and your cheerleaders have decided to invite other school organizations to help with the pep rally, set up times to discuss ideas with the sponsors of the organizations and to meet with members of each group to make sure they are ready. Some schools encourage representatives from different clubs to be involved in a skit or a class competition of some sort. Some pep rallies feature special announcements such as outstanding achievement in academics, forensics, drama, other sports, or service projects. The pep rally provides an excellent opportunity to validate any student or group who has been successful and does not need to be limited to a focus on one game or one sport.

Communicating With the Student Body

The most common ways to announce an upcoming pep rally to the student body are through posters in the hallways, banners in the cafeteria, announcements on the intercom, an article in the student newspaper, flyers, or by asking teachers to write the information on the chalkboard in the classrooms. Cheerleaders, coaches, and team members should also personally promote the pep rally.

Ways to generate interest in the pep rally are to advertise a "mystery guest," talk about a new spirit award for the class competition, include teachers in a special pie throwing or water balloon tossing contest, focus on the importance of the upcoming game, or feature an "ugly legs contest." Each pep rally needs to be unique and fun and exciting. The success begins with pep rally promotion and thorough communication preceding the event.

Working With School Administrators and Faculty

You and your captains need to work closely with an administrator, usually an assistant principal or athletic director (or both). You will need to develop and write up the pep rally plan at least a week in advance and ask the principal, assistant principal, or athletic director for final approval. Once that is done, make sure each faculty member receives information about the upcoming pep rally, including the exact time schedule, at least a week in advance. Faculty members are usually informed through the use of the faculty mailboxes. Coordinate the exact requirements with your administrators.

Not only do I feel that administrators should be informed and involved, I believe they should maintain control during a pep rally that needs leadership. I once visited a high school pep rally where the classes were competing for a spirit award. I witnessed many examples of very poor sportsmanship (such as booing, throwing newspaper on the floor during another class's skit, and shouting to drown out the speakers). At no time during the pep rally did an administrator or faculty member step forward and remind the class representatives that poor sportsmanship would count against them in the judging. Therefore, the class that "won" was one of the classes who had displayed unacceptable behavior. The administrators should have stepped forward and not only stopped the behavior, but prevented validation of such poor sportsmanship.

Great Pep Rally Ideas

Great pep rallies start with great planning. A Pep Rally Planning Sheet can help you get all of the details listed. Figure 10.1 provides a sample of the information that needs to be compiled when planning for the pep rally.

In order to schedule everything into your allotted time, you will need to break down each element of the pep rally into time frames. Figure 10.2 shows how to allocate the time for a 30-minute pep rally.

Pep Rally Planning Sheet

Date today ______________ Cheerleading coach ______________

Date of pep rally ______________ Time of pep rally ______________

Location ______________ Opponent ______________

Mascot ______________ Colors ______________

Theme ______________

MC/Speaker ______________

Cheers ______________

Chants ______________

Music ______________

Dance ______________

Posters or banners ______________

Props ______________

Equipment ______________

Skit outline (use back of this form)

Class competition ______________

Special plans ______________

____

Individuals and groups participating ______________

Administration and faculty to notify:

____ Cheer coach ____ Principal

____ Athletic director ____ Team coach

____ Band director

Figure 10.1 Pep rally planning sheet.

Timing of elements can be lengthened or shortened depending on how long you have. Also, events can be substituted or deleted depending on the exact schedule of your pep rally. A word of caution: Pep rallies are usually more effective if they are not over 30 minutes long. It's difficult to sustain a high energy level for pep rallies that are longer. It's better to keep the pep rally at frenzy pitch for a shorter duration than to let it get bogged down.

THE PRIDE AND THE SPIRIT

I once judged a series of outstanding pep rallies for a national competition sponsored by a beverage company. I was flown to five locations across the country to judge these pep rallies and I was constantly amazed at the community involvement in these events! The pep rallies that I witnessed embodied the true meaning of high school spirit. Each school was meticulously decorated, from the hallways to the classrooms to the cafeteria. The gymnasi-

Pep Rally Event Schedule

5 min	Band plays as students enter gymnasium
2 min	Cheerleaders lead a few short spirit chants
2 min	Welcome and general announcements
2 min	Short cheer
4 min	Coach talks, introduces captains
1 min	Good luck or sportsmanship cheer
5 min	Skit
3 min	Dance
4 min	Class competition or contest
2 min	Final announcements
	Band plays fight song as students leave

Figure 10.2 Sample pep rally event schedule.

ums were totally covered in posters and banners, the volume was thunderous, and the spirit was fever-pitch. Bands played, cheerleaders cheered, drill teams danced. Community business leaders supported the festivities with parades, floats, signs, and skits. What I remember most, besides the noise, the color, and the red carpet treatment, was the electricity in the air as students, faculty, and community came together to present the pride and the spirit that encompassed their school.

Tips for Successful Pep Rallies

Your pep rally can supercharge your entire school! If you are organized in advance, you can keep a quick, spirited pace. Make sure that everything runs on time. Keep the time down to 20-30 minutes (although some skits or class competitions are long, sometimes the band plays more than just at the beginning and end, and the coach can get carried away talking, etc.)

Before the pep rally starts, make sure the sound equipment is in good working order. Everyone needs to hear everything. The person speaking on the microphone should speak loudly and clearly. If possible, use some sort of signs or props in the skit or for crowd involvement chants. Make sure your mascot is highly visible during the pep rally to help keep everyone pumped up. Try to include the faculty or an administrator in some way (in a skit or contest if possible) because students really enjoy this.

Remember why you are having the pep rally: to boost the team and to encourage students to attend the game in support of the athletic program. Stay focused on presenting an organized, spirited, and fun pep rally. Be sure to thank everyone who helped on the pep rally (ask your cheerleaders to write thank you notes).

Pep Rally Activities

You and your cheerleaders can liven up the pep rally by planning fun and exciting special activities, such as a contest, to take place during the rally. Each pep rally needs to have a theme, a special surprise, or a creative idea that makes it different from any other pep rally. Here are some ideas to help make your pep rallies memorable, fun, and exciting.

PEP RALLY ACTIVITIES

1. Free Throw Contest. During the pep rally, have a free throw contest between members of the team and some of the teachers. The losers receive a cream pie in the face.

2. Mock Rock. Ask representatives from clubs or student groups to put together their own "MTV" performances by doing a lip sync of recorded music by a popular music group. Judge on costumes, lip sync ability, and overall performance.

3. Minicontests. These can be done during the pep rally using both students and teachers. Examples are Jell-O slurping, balloon blowing, cola guzzling, marshmallow stuffing.

4. School Olympics. Examples include water balloon volleyball, using a sheet to toss the water balloon; egg toss, with rows moving farther back after each throw; tricycle, wheelbarrow, or potato sack races; a scavenger hunt put together by teachers; or an obstacle course around the gym floor.

5. Smile Contest. Have a contest involving students, teachers, players, and coaches, where an "official panel of judges" will select the best smile. The prize could be a giant toothbrush.

6. Red Carpet Treatment. Roll out a red carpet for the coaches and players to walk on as they walk to their seats in the gymnasium before the pep rally starts.

7. Giant Posters. Make huge posters or banners with the words to the cheers and chants on them to display at the pep rally so everyone can support the team by yelling with the cheerleaders.

8. Jump for Victory. Have a jumping contest during the pep rally where the cheerleaders demonstrate a jump, and a coach, player, or teacher must copy it.

9. Airplane Toss. Distribute a piece of paper to students and have them write their name on it, assemble a paper airplane, and sail the airplanes to the middle of a giant circle of pompons on the gym floor. The planes that land in the center of the circle win a special spirit prize.

10. Parent Squad. Invite the parents of the players to the pep rally wearing their son's or daughter's warm-up jacket and pants. They can do exercises and play basketball with an administrator as their coach.

11. Wrap Up a Victory. Select four or five players to represent the team. Have a race to see which cheerleader (or class representative) can wrap a roll of toilet paper around a player first.

12. Surprise Cheerleaders. Well in advance, have each cheerleader choose a little girl or boy from the community to be a cheerleader for the day. Work with the children and get them ready for the pep rally, keeping their performance a secret. At the beginning of the pep rally, have them run into the gym, doing somersaults, jumps, and chants. They can also lead a cheer or perform a dance routine.

13. Booster Club Pep Rally. Ask the adult Booster Club members to conduct the pep rally. Work closely with them to plan all aspects.

14. Skit Competition. Team captains and coaches are asked to create a skit for the pep rally using eight members of their team. There should be a time limit of five minutes total, and the skit should be judged on creativity, humor, length, costumes, and punch line.

15. Nicknames. Make up a nickname or a slogan for each player that refers to the upcoming game.

16. Kick the Football Contest. Players line up in front of tees with footballs, which they are supposed to kick. Blindfold the players and have them try to kick the football (which you have removed from the tee).

17. Cool Contest. Have the players sit on blocks of ice during the pep rally. The one that sits there the longest is known as "Mr. Cool" or "Ms. Cool."

18. Dreaming of a Victory. Borrow the pajamas of the players and model them during the pep rally. If someone doesn't own any, wear a large barrel or sheet.

19. Sports Quiz. Contestants answer questions about your school's sports teams. The players can make up the questions. Losers get a pie in the face.

OUR SPIRIT IS FLYING HIGH

It's such a magical sight: hundreds of paper airplanes in flight at precisely the same moment. For our theme, "Our Spirit is Flying High," we decided to have a paper airplane contest in the gym at the end of our pep rally. Everyone was instructed to bring a paper airplane to the pep rally, with the pilot's name clearly written somewhere on it. The cheerleaders made a circle with pompons in the middle of the gym and this was the target point. After, "On your mark, get set, fly," the air was filled with lightweight paper airplanes, all heading for the pompon target. The winning pilots were announced and presented with donated gift certificates.

Ongoing Ideas for School Spirit

School spirit does not need to be solely dependent on the win/loss record of your athletic teams, although it may seem that way. There are many ongoing spirit ideas that can build tradition and pride in the school unrelated to the score at the end of the game. I will discuss ideas to develop community support, increase student involvement, and validate all student accomplishment.

Developing Community Support

The schools with the best spirit usually have excellent community support. There are three main reasons for this:

- There are many faithful alumni still in the community who have children attending the school.
- The school has achieved some outstanding accomplishments and the community is proud of the reputation.
- The school is new and everyone is excited about starting new traditions.

One of the ways to develop good community support is to make sure that the community is informed about the events. Most schools have a Booster Club that supports the athletic programs and serves as the springboard to the rest of the community. The Booster Club needs to be included in special pep rally plans, Homecoming, and athletic banquets.

To validate the community's support, I would like to recommend that for at least one pep rally you have a "Community Appreciation Day" and include representatives from businesses and service organizations in your rally. One way to feature these representatives is to have them either dress up, bring signs, or ride in small floats for a parade around the gymnasium floor. This show of support at the pep rally has a tremendous effect on the team and the school.

Another way to get the community involved with supporting the school is to print a WE SUPPORT OUR TEAM poster, inviting businesses and organizations to purchase low priced ads for this poster. The poster should also feature pictures of the teams and a complete schedule of all athletic events.

A community newsletter, a column in the PTA newsletter or bulletin, or articles in the local newspaper are also ways to get the word out about the events at your school.

Community Windows

When you are targeting a specific game, you can place specialized spirit signs such as the following in the windows of your community businesses.

Bank: Our interest is in the (mascot)! Lay your money on the (mascot)!
Car Wash: Wash 'em out! Victory is a clean sweep!
Real Estate: Invest in (mascot) pride!
Hardware Store: Paint the town (school colors)! Build your spirit!
Beauty Shop: Victory is beautiful! (Mascot) have style!
Cleaners: Clean 'em out! We're impressed with the (mascot)!
Shoe Store: Defeat 'em! Stomp 'em! Our victory is a shoe-in!
Ice Cream Store: I scream for victory!

Pizza Place: Anyway you slice it, we're going to win!
Bowling Alley: Strike with power! Bowl 'em over!
Car Dealer: (Mascot) is in the driver's seat! Steer us to a victory!
Fabric Store: Sew up a victory!
Lawyer's Office: We've got an iron clad defense!
Restaurant: Victory is our specialty of the day!
Library: Check out a victory! We're Gone With The Win!
Business: We're the type to win! Compute a victory!

Increasing Student Involvement

One of the best ways to increase student involvement is to have class competitions throughout the year. Some class competitions are held during pep rallies, and some are ongoing throughout the year. These class competitions are intended to increase spirit and not to increase animosity between the classes. These contest ideas should be fun and spirited, and aimed to support the school in a positive way. Here are some ideas to use for class competitions.

IDEAS FOR CLASS COMPETITIONS

1. Decorate a Mascot. Representatives of each class form a team. Each team is given newspaper, crepe paper, construction paper, tape, and scissors and has five minutes to decorate one of their members as a class mascot.

2. Bubble Gum Contest. Each class and the faculty should be represented. Give each person five pieces of bubble gum. After they have chewed the gum for a few minutes, they compete to see who can blow the biggest bubble.

3. Juggling Contest. This contest involves three representatives from each class. The first person juggles three apples. The second person juggles three bananas. The third and final person juggles three eggs.

4. Penny Hunt. Class representatives hunt for pennies in ten pounds of flour.

5. Tape Off. Each class has a different colored tape. Students buy inches of tape for one cent per inch. Each class tries to have the longest length of tape around the gym walls, down the hallway, or on the cafeteria ceiling.

6. Poster Contest. This class competition needs a set of impartial judges. Each class makes a specific number of spirit posters and places them in the cafeteria or down hallways. Categories include class spirit, school spirit, originality, sportsmanship, and neatness.

7. We Can Do It. Each class collects aluminum pop cans to show that "United we CAN do it!" Have a contest for the best sculpture made out of the cans, build a giant mascot out of them, or make your school letters.

8. Chair Chants. Have chants taped to the underneath side of chairs. Have a relay where one person from each class runs to the other end of the gym where the chairs are placed. They sit down, get the envelope with the chant, run back, and start the chant in front of their class. The class that starts the chant first wins.

9. Original Cheer Contest. Each class sends a representative to draw five to eight words out of a box. Then each class must make up a chant or cheer out of those words. The first class to do a chant or cheer with the words is the winner.

10. Class Presidents Lead Cheers. Each class has a specific word, such as Go...Lions...Beat...Tigers. The president of the class leads their class with their word. Faculty members can select the loudest class.

11. Stomp 'Em. Representatives of each class pile up their shoes at one end of the gym. Mix them up. At the sound of a buzzer, they all run out to find their own shoes. The class that finishes putting all of their shoes on first wins.

12. It's in the Bag. Have a contest with class representatives changing clothes in a zipped-up sleeping bag.

13. Spirit Section. Give each class a certain section of the gym to decorate for a pep rally. Faculty members and administrators could judge which class does the best job.

14. Class Choice Day. During Spirit Week, have one day where each class selects a different theme of their own. This could become a class competition to see which class has the highest percentage of students dressed in the theme.

Ideas for Spirit Day Themes

One way to get students involved in school spirit is to have a Spirit Week that precedes a game. Each day has a special theme, and students dress up for the theme. The theme days show the team and coaches how much the students support the school and the sport.

- Denim Day
- Hat Day
- Overall Spirit Day (wear overalls)
- Surfer Day
- Inside Out Day
- Sunglasses Day
- School Color Day
- Pajama Day
- Sixties Day
- Kindergarten Day
- Boxer Short Day
- MTV Day

Student involvement in school spirit activities can be increased through more publicity about what's going on. Make announcements over the school intercom system about upcoming events, hang posters in the hallways, or write a weekly column in the school newspaper geared specifically toward school spirit activities. Students can be asked to get involved in a more direct way by filling out a School Spirit Questionnaire (see figure 13.2) in a classroom or helping to hang posters and banners.

Validating All Student Accomplishment

Whether athletes or not, all students need to be validated for achievement. Some schools honor students periodically with articles in the school newspaper, city newspaper, announcements on the intercom system, recognition during pep rallies, banquets, or special ceremonies. Your cheerleaders need to make sure they keep up with individual student accomplishment and assist in it being honored. They can each specialize in a particular class, specific clubs or organizations, or a particular sport team to break down the task.

I know of a school that validates student success with Y.E.S. buttons (You're Extra Special). The buttons are worn with pride, and the students are honored with certificates, articles in the newspaper, and recognition at school events.

Another way to validate all students is to establish a Wall of Fame in the cafeteria or a main hallway. Information and photographs are featured here so that students in the school can appreciate outstanding achievement.

Your cheerleaders will have a better chance of uniting the school with spirit and pride if they make sure that students are honored and validated for success in any area of endeavor.

Summary

Following are some important points to consider for building school spirit:

- Pep rallies can make a dramatic impact on school spirit and student support.
- Organization and communication are the cornerstone of pep rally success.
- Most pep rallies have the same basic components, with some variations possible, such as band involvement, cheers and chants, coach talk, skit, class competitions, dance routine, and fight song.
- The Pep Club needs to be involved in the pep rally, serving as the catalyst for the other students.
- Communicate in advance with the band director and other school organizations that are involved in the pep rally.
- Ways to communicate about the pep rally are through posters in the hallways, announcements on the intercom, an article in the school newspaper, or flyers.
- Organizers of the pep rally need to work closely with a school administrator and obtain approval on the exact schedule.

- Great pep rallies start with great planning. Fill out a planning sheet in advance to get everything organized.
- Pep rallies are usually more effective if they are between 20 and 30 minutes long.
- Make sure the pep rally adheres to the time limits set for each event.
- Each pep rally needs to have a theme, special surprise, or creative idea that makes it fun and exciting.
- Effective community support requires good communication.
- Athletic programs are usually supported by an involved Booster Club.
- A "Community Appreciation Day" can help develop good community support.
- One of the best ways to increase student involvement is to have class competitions.
- Whether athletes or not, all students need to be validated for outstanding achievement.
- Your cheerleaders need to make sure they keep up with individual student accomplishment and assist in it being honored.

Chapter 11

Cheerleading Camps and Competitions

A cheerleader's life doesn't always revolve around school spirit and the upcoming game. Many cheerleaders attend summer camp, and some enter competitions. Both camp and competitions are filled with challenge, opportunity, and fun.

Summer camps originated in the 1950s and competitions for cheerleaders started soon after. Cheerleading squads have been competing against each other at the local or state level for a long time. National competition for cheerleaders is a relatively recent development, starting on the collegiate level in the late 1970s and spreading to the high school and junior high school level. As more and more cheerleaders attended summer camps, interest in competitions increased. The popularity of cheerleading competition has continued to grow, largely due to nationally televised competitions, and attending summer camp has become a tradition. In this chapter I will provide information about selecting a summer camp and on how to prepare mentally and physically for competition. I will also discuss the benefits of cheer competitions and considerations for the event itself.

Benefits of Attending Summer Camp

I highly recommend that you and your cheerleaders attend a summer camp because I believe there are many benefits to be gained from the experience. Living together in a dorm, you will encounter many opportunities to develop friendships, increase squad unity, and increase confidence. You have more time to plan, talk, laugh, eat, practice, and share. During camp, your cheerleaders will need to work together while calling on their personal levels of dedication, discipline, organization, and leadership. Cheerleading camp will give your squad opportunities to meet challenges, work through them, and build additional personal and cheering skills.

Beyond the benefits of being together as a group, the camp instructional program (cheers, chants, dances, stunts, pep rally ideas, school spirit ideas, fundraising ideas, etc.) offers an advanced education in cheering. The staff members at your camp are usually highly skilled and dedicated college and university cheerleaders who will make a positive impact by how they teach and how they relate personally. You will be meeting (and learning from) coaches and cheerleaders from other schools at the same time. And if the camp offers awards for competition, your squad can strive for special recognition.

Summer camp memories will live forever in your mind and your heart. It is an experience of a lifetime.

Selecting a Summer Camp

Summer camp! Thousands of cheerleaders across the country get goose bumps just thinking about it. And this summer will be no different as they pack their bags and head for one of the most exciting weeks of their lives.

Selecting the right summer camp is very important. But figuring out what is just right for you and your squad can be a daunting task. Some important areas to consider are location, cost, and the cheerleading company.

Location

1. What do we know about the facilities at this camp? For instance, is the dorm air-conditioned? Will sessions be held inside or outside?
2. Do we have transportation to and from this location?
3. Has anyone attended any type of camp there in the past?
4. What have we heard about this camp in the past?
5. What type of supervision does the dorm provide?
6. How safe is this area, town, or city?
7. Do we live close enough to stay at home and commute to the camp?

Cost

1. Does the price of this camp seem reasonable, and can everyone afford it?
2. What fundraising projects can be organized to help pay for the camp?
3. How much of a deposit needs to be sent in with the registration?
4. How much is the total cost of the camp (room, board, tuition), and when is all of the money due?
5. Is there a deadline to sign up for the camp?
6. How does this price compare with other camps in our area?
7. How does this price compare with other camps in our state?

The Cheerleading Company

1. What do we already know about this company?
2. What is the general philosophy of this company?
3. What style of cheerleading does this company teach?
4. What have we heard about this company's staff members?
5. How does this company organize its camps, conduct the sessions, handle evaluation and competition?
6. What kinds of awards are presented?
7. Does this company provide teaching materials at the camp?
8. Does the camp schedule stress all of the important areas in effective cheerleading?
9. Does the program provide time for private coaching and intensive practice?
10. Does this program provide all of the things we need to get out of a camp?
11. Is camp insurance offered?
12. Will there be an athletic trainer at the camp?
13. What will the instructor to student ratio be during our session?

You need to discuss all of these areas with your cheerleaders and their parents before the final decision is made. Some squads from the same school decide to attend different camps so they can share new ideas when they get back. Some prefer attending the same camp to help improve intersquad communication and unity. Some schools host a "private camp," where a company sends staff members to the school. A private camp company can specialize in exactly what that school wants to learn and not teach anything that the school does not want or need. Be sure to discuss all of the options before making the decision about camp.

Summer camp can provide your squad with skills and technique improvement, which can be further developed as you help them prepare for competition. The camp experience is extremely important in building the cohesiveness of your squad.

Should Cheerleaders Compete?

There are times when you may get frustrated and begin to doubt your decision to work with your cheerleaders in preparation for a competition. You may even have some parents and administrators who will challenge your decision. After all, the purpose of cheerleading is not to grab the spotlight, but to guide the spotlight that shines on the team. Should cheerleaders compete? My answer is "Yes," if they want to.

Cheerleaders can gain valuable experiences by participating in competition. The preparation and the competition can help your cheerleaders appreciate and assimilate values that will influence their lives forever, including the following:

- Working together toward a common goal will help them learn the value of teamwork.
- Making a commitment to prepare and participate will help them develop discipline in other areas of their lives as well.
- Learning how to set short-term and long-term goals, both individually and as a team, will benefit your cheerleaders in whatever they do.
- Participating in a competition helps your cheerleaders learn to accept victory with joy and defeat with dignity.
- Small, sequential successes during the preparation process will help your squad members gain self-respect, confidence, and personal power.
- Trading ideas with other squads provides an excellent opportunity for you and your cheerleaders to broaden your repertoire.
- Getting to know cheerleaders from other schools promotes good sportsmanship and mutual understanding.
- Traveling and sight-seeing can provide positive experiences and memories.
- Preparing for competition can help unite a school and a community toward a common goal.
- Cheerleading competition often helps develop advanced technical cheer skills and provide the foundation for individuals to reach higher performance and athletic goals.

If your squad decides to compete, keep in mind that each practice, each performance, and each experience in front of the judges can help prepare your squad members for life's challenges in adult circumstances. They will gain practice in managing their time, mentally preparing for a performance, forming group cohesion, and handling disappointment and victory. Your role should always be to reinforce lifetime values, choices, and skills. True winning is not determined by a score sheet, a trophy, or a photograph in a newspaper. The real winners show grace in victory, poise and perseverance in defeat. For instance, your squad can congratulate the winners, decide to try again, and compare themselves only to their own improvement. Set a good example for your cheerleaders by validating positive behavior and talking in advance about how to handle disappointment.

When it's time for the focus to shift from support to spotlight, keep your cheerleaders grounded in what is truly important: preparation through personal commitment, teamwork, and sportsmanship. The mental and physical preparation will have immeasurable results.

Mental Preparation for Competition

Competition requires a total mind shift from a philosophy of support to one of spotlight. When the time comes to take the floor as competitors, your cheerleaders need to be mentally prepared to handle the pressure of competition, the anticipation of success, and the possibility of defeat. Mental preparation by cheerleaders depends largely on the attitude of the coach, the support of their families, and the attitude of the cheerleaders themselves.

Coach Attitude

You will need to be sincerely dedicated to helping your cheerleaders do their absolute best as they prepare. Since the practices for competition are usually extra work for everyone, your attitude about giving more of your time to your cheerleaders needs to be positive and pumped. Here is a sampling of what you can do to help your cheerleaders prepare mentally:

- Build self-confidence through positive feedback. When you are giving constructive criticism to your squad, always tell them what they are doing well.
- Keep competition in its proper perspective; do not allow it to become more important than support of the athletic programs. Of course, your squad will want to win, but take time to discuss the other benefits to being involved in a competition (increased skill level and unity, for example). Remind them that they are already winners because they have been chosen to represent the school.
- Use mental imagery during practice to help your cheerleaders visualize a flawless performance. You can help them learn the power of their own minds through guided imagery exercises.
- Be sensitive to signs that competition might be causing stress, and ease the pressure by bringing more fun activities to practices.
- Surprise your squad occasionally with special snacks, beverages, or spirit gifts with positive slogans.

Your attitude and reaction to your cheerleaders will have a profound effect on them, whether at practice or at the actual competition. Open, honest communication during the preparation process is crucial to your squad's success. The "will to prepare to win" is a mental mind-set that needs to be adopted by you and your cheerleaders. You will also need to spend some time discussing how to handle disappointment. If your squad loses a competition, let them know that they are not failures as individuals and that life will go on.

ROLE MODEL

She was a friend of mine so I knew her face and mannerisms well. She had dedicated many years to working with cheerleaders, and I knew she had recently been working even harder with them. From across the room I could see her when the places were announced. When her squad did not win, I could tell that she was suffering excruciating disappointment. However, she appeared poised, calm, and positive. The squad huddled together briefly, then poised, calm, and positive, they went over to congratulate the first-place winners. I was not surprised. She demonstrated something I have known for a long time: like coach, like squad.

Family Support

Cheerleading squads who have decided to compete spend many more hours practicing than squads who do not compete. The additional practice times mean less time for family responsibilities, work demands, and friends. The support and understanding of family and friends is crucial to the success of the competition experience. Family and friends need to feel they are an integral part of the excitement as the squad prepares for competition. They care about your squad members and can lend constant support from the stands.

Winning is an attitude that is shared by everyone who mentally prepares for the competition, whether they are on the floor or in the stands. I have attended many competitions where I witnessed the solid support of family and friends, who usually show up wearing matching shirts, carrying signs, and bringing gifts for their cheerleaders. The anticipation of success, the anxiety of performance, and the culmination of emotion is shared equally among cheerleaders and those who love them.

Cheerleader Attitude

Deciding to compete must be a group decision. The mental, physical, and personal demands are outside the normal, day-to-day lifestyle in the life of a teenager, so commitment is the key to the success of the preparation. Some of your cheerleaders might need to spend time during the preparation process talking about their feelings, discussing their personal challenges, and helping each other through the rough times. The added stress of extra practices and strenuous competitive performance (plus homework, jobs, family obligations) may cause problems that differ from support cheering. Some schools have a separate squad for competition, which requires a separate tryout. This can make it easier for the individual who is not ready for the challenges of competition or who has different interests.

Stay informed about what is going on within the squad as a group and as individuals. Some things to notice are personality conflicts, flare-ups, arguments, complaining, half-hearted contribution, and absenteeism—symptoms of possible burn-out or stress. I recommend a personal meeting with every cheerleader sometime before the actual competition to make sure that each individual is focused and having fun.

Physical Preparation for Competition

Besides preparing mentally, each squad member must prepare physically for the demands of competition. The cheerleaders on your squad will need to make an honest commitment to personal conditioning, strengthening, and training as they prepare for competition. They will need to stay in shape by conditioning with aerobic and anaerobic workouts if the competition periods occur outside the regular cheerleading seasons. They will need to continue to build strong ankles, knees, wrists, and major muscle groups to help alleviate injuries and soreness during the competition practice periods. And they will need to attend all practices so that they may competently simulate the actual competition experience from beginning to end.

The level of personal commitment to preparing physically for competition will determine the skill level attained by your cheerleaders. You may want to set preparation goals specifically for the competition, such as individual goals to improve a skill needed in the routine (a perfect toe touch for example) and squad skill goals that are crucial to the effectiveness of the routine (a flawless dance segment or pyramid). You may want to plan a special incentive for the squad if they meet their preparation goals: for example, a party, a special performance for the school or community, or any other outside motivation that may help spark your cheerleaders.

As you coach your cheerleaders toward their physical preparation goals, you may need to alter your day-to-day practices to accommodate competition goals. For instance, you may want to introduce parts of the competition routine at various times during the season and work these ideas into regular cheering responsibilities. Your coaching techniques will be determined by the actual competition routine, which will probably consist of cheers, chants, dancing, and stunts. You could focus on a few key pyramids or work on a special tumbling pass so that you will be ready to put them into the routine at a later time. You will need to develop additional dancing skills for the competition routine if you do not perform dance routines during your regular cheerleading seasons. Each component (cheers, chants, transitions, dance, pyramids, ending, etc.) of the competition routine needs to be coached individually, and then put together for the final routine.

Many coaches of competition squads have professional coaches help them plan, teach, and coach the competition routine. If this is the route that you decide to take with your squad, make sure that the professional coach conducts the sessions within the parameters of your own coaching philosophy. You do not want a private coach to put mental or physical stress on your squad members. Obviously you need to attend all of these training sessions and screen everything that is done.

Preparing for the Competition Routine

Sometimes the practices for competition occur during practices for games. If this is the case, try to keep the two separate in some way so that the cheerleaders understand that their primary responsibility is to support the school. Competition cheering is an "extra" and needs to be treated as a reward. If you have a support squad and a competitive squad, they may each have their own practice times and locations.

Preparing physically for competition needs to be a continuation of your existing program, not a departure from it. Your philosophy of coaching should still be in effect as you help prepare your squad to take on a new challenge. Helping your cheerleaders prepare physically for competition can be quite demanding on you because of the time element, the focused attention to specialized conditioning, strengthening, and training, and the added stress of preparing for a judged performance. Try to plan some extra fun and variety at your practices so that your cheerleaders will not become exhausted or burned out.

As you and your squad prepare physically for the competition, be sure to discuss the following areas.

1. Go over the judging form together to make sure that your squad is strong in all of the judging areas. Is the form "weighted" in one direction or another? Are stunts worth more points proportionally than cheers or chants? Closely analyze the judging areas and evaluate your routine using this form as often as possible.

2. Plan a routine that is slightly under the time limit to allow you some "recovery" time if something doesn't go just right. Remember to constantly time the routine during practices to make sure you are within the time limit.

3. If music is being used, consider having it professionally recorded and mixed. Also, screen the music for undesirable lyrics.

4. If you are incorporating pyramids or tumbling, make sure that they are flawless. Do not let your cheerleaders add stunts to the routine at the last minute or perform stunts they are not ready for. I have seen squads overextend themselves in this area who have regretted it later because they could not pull it off during the competition. It's better to do something that's a little easier that you can do well than to risk injury or embarrassment by missing a stunt.

5. Make sure your cheerleaders are performing within the prescribed safety rules for the competition, and for your school. If you are in doubt about a stunt you are adding to your routine, check in the National Federation's *High School Spirit Rules Book* or with your competition hosts for a ruling.

Types of Competitions

A variety of competitions are available through cheerleading companies, state high school associations, and cheerleading coaches' associations. Familiarize yourself with the different options so you can choose the one that best fits your program.

Summer Camp Competitions

A lot of the private cheerleading companies offer the opportunity to compete at camp against the other squads who attend the same camp. Professional instructors evaluate the squad on special forms, rating them on specific cheerleading areas. Sometimes the instructors provide written comments or criticisms. At the end of the camp, squads are often announced in rank order, based on the numbers they received on the judging forms. Some squads are singled out as being in the "Top 10" or as achieving a special recognition award (a ribbon, certificate, or trophy).

Some summer camp companies provide the opportunity to compete at a regional level in order to qualify for a national competition. The regional competition usually involves cheerleaders from more than one state being invited to compete at a central location. The process will vary from company to company, but basically the squads are selected for the quality of accumulated performances during the camp. The national competition represents the top squads from different states that have attended summer camps hosted by that company.

State Competitions

Some state high school associations sanction a state cheerleading competition. For instance, the Missouri Cheerleading Coaches Association hosts a state competition that is sanctioned by the Missouri State High School Activities Association. This means that the competition is organized in a manner similar to the state football or basketball competitions. It also means that the cheerleaders would be able to attend the competition as official representatives of your school, the school can provide transportation, and the cheerleaders are allowed to miss school for travel time. These stipulations will vary from state to state, so make sure you get the details that apply to your state. Check with your state high school association to see if your state sanctions a state competition.

Private Competitions

A private competition can be one that is hosted by a dance or gymnastics studio, a local school, or a college or university. Some state fairs offer a competition as part of their activities. College and university cheerleaders often host a cheerleading competition for their local high schools and junior highs or middle schools. Sometimes cheerleading competitions are hosted in the parking lot or central arena of a shopping center. Most state high school associations do not allow their cheerleaders to become involved in this type of competition. Steer clear of situations where the cheering surfaces and other conditions are not conducive to safe cheering.

Individual Competitions

Some cheerleaders have the opportunity to compete for individual recognition during a summer camp experience, with the possibility of continuing on to a national competition at a later point in time. Cheerleaders at summer camps are also sometimes selected to perform for a nationally televised Bowl game or parade. Another way that an individual can qualify for individual competition is to send a videotape to a national cheerleading company.

Open Competitions

Cheerleaders, as a squad or as individuals, can qualify at a camp, clinic, or by videotape to compete in an "open" competition, which usually means that any cheerleader or squad may enter and attendance at a specific company's camp or clinic is not a prerequisite. Some open competitions are by invitation only where you respond to a mailing or personal request.

Competition Details

Before you and your cheerleaders decide to participate in a cheerleading competition, you should gather as much information as possible about the competition procedure itself as well as about the credibility of the competition hosts. Try to talk to other coaches who have attended the competition you are thinking about attending. You will also need to evaluate the facilities of the competition location, the competition rules, the safety rules, and the emergency procedures. Make sure you understand the judging procedure and the judging form itself. Also, find out what kinds of awards will be presented.

Competition Procedure

Whether you qualify at camp, qualify through a regional competition, or respond to a mailing about a local or open competition, you should receive a precompetition information packet at least one month in advance of the event. This information packet should contain a map of the facility, time of competition, exact competition site within the facility, list of safety rules, sample judging form, squad classifications or divisions, and information about lodging if needed. Competition classifications or divisions are usually determined by number of squad members or school enrollment. Other divisions can include music or no music, all girl or coed, or all-star (squad members do not represent a school). After the competition, you should be able to receive your judging forms, which can be distributed at the event or mailed.

On the day of the event, arrive with the squad and make sure they are on time to each event. Set a good example of good sportsmanship, supervise all activities, attend coach meetings, have your music cued, and have your emergency medical permission forms with you at all times.

Facilities

When you are evaluating the facilities of the competition location, safety must be your foremost concern. Your cheerleaders should cheer on a wooden floor (such as a basketball court), with sufficient space to safely perform the routine, and with adequate lighting. There should be a warm-up area, with mats if possible. You may wish to find out about the availability of a locked room for personal items, the videotaping policy, and the service of a sound technician during the competition.

Competition Rules

Cheerleading companies who host national competitions have their own safety and routine rules for competition. If the safety rules for the competition allow illegal stunts according to your state high school association (or the National Federation's *High School Spirit Rules Book*) you should follow your state's rules. Cheerleading coaches associations that host state competitions follow the state rules. The routine rules, such as time limits, boundaries (cheering space), and components (stunts, no stunts, music, no music) are determined by the competition host.

Medical Provisions

All competition personnel, including coaches, should know what to do in case of injury, illness, or emergency. It is important that the competition you attend provides a certified athletic trainer and other medical personnel during the entire competition. In some cases, a training room may be available during the competition. Also, supplies should be provided.

Judging

In order for you to respect the judges' decisions, you will need to respect their expertise. Read their qualifications, checking for years of experience in judging and coaching, plus experience teaching at camps or clinics as a professional instructor. Your squad will probably be judged by three to five judges with varying experience. The same judges will judge all of the squads in a division. You may also have a judge for penalties (penalty points are usually given for illegal stunts, for going overtime, or for stepping out of bounds) and a judge for level of difficulty (for stunts only). When you receive a copy of the judging form, study the point distribution (100 points possible is common). Here is an example of the areas that are traditionally judged. However, the actual wording and point scale will differ for each competition.

- *Cheering Skills:* jumps, stunts
- *Cheer Execution:* motions, timing, voice
- *Crowd Appeal:* personality projection, spirit, appearance, showmanship
- *Overall Effectiveness:* transitions, creativity, routine dynamics
- *Dance:* choreography, timing, creativity, impact
- *Level of Difficulty:* stunts representing skill levels

Evaluate your squad's skills in the light of the judging form: Do you think they are ready for competition?

Awards

The awards given at each competition will differ. Usually squads are ranked by places (first, second, third, etc.) within each division (the actual number of places and awards differ with each competition). The places are determined by total number of points. Sometimes special awards are given for originality, choreography, spirit, leadership, and dance. The awards are usually ribbons, certificates, plaques, and trophies (and sometimes a combination, such as individual ribbons for squad members and a trophy for the squad). When you are considering whether to compete, the information on awards will help you get a clearer picture as to how many squads will be rewarded and if you think your squad will have a chance to receive an award.

Summary

Here are the key points to consider when evaluating cheerleading camps and competitions:

- Summer cheerleading camp has been a tradition since the 1950s, and the popularity of cheerleading competition has grown with it.
- Cheerleading squads have been competing against each other at the local and state level for a long time now.
- National cheerleading competition started on the collegiate level and

spread to the high school and junior high levels, largely due to televised cheer competitions.

- Some of the benefits of attending a cheerleading camp are learning new ideas to use during the school year and developing squad unity.
- When deciding which summer camp to attend, evaluate information about the location of the camp, the cost, and the cheerleading company conducting the camp.
- Cheerleaders need to be mentally prepared to handle the pressure of competition, the anticipation of success, and the possibility of defeat.
- Mental preparation by cheerleaders for competition depends largely on the attitude of the coach, the support of their families, and the attitude of the cheerleaders themselves.
- One of a coach's most basic responsibilities is to help build self-confidence in your cheerleaders through positive feedback.
- The cheerleaders on your squad will need to make an honest commitment to personal conditioning, strengthening, and training as they prepare for competition.
- Sometimes you may need to use specialized coaching techniques, to be determined by the demands of the competition routine itself.
- As you prepare for competition, go over the judging form to make sure that you are strong in all of the judging areas.
- The process of preparation for competition provides a valuable learning experience for each individual on your squad.
- Cheerleaders can gain valuable experiences by participating in competition, which requires teamwork, commitment, goal setting, self-respect, confidence, sportsmanship, and skill development.
- Evaluate the level of professionalism of the competition hosts, which will be evident by the facilities, competition procedures, medical provisions, competition rules, judging, and awards.
- Some professional cheerleading companies offer excellent opportunities for competition experience.
- Many competitions are sanctioned by or administered by the state high school association or by a state cheerleading coaches association.

Part V

Coaching Evaluation

Chapter 12

© Thomas J. Benincas, Jr.

Evaluating Cheerleaders' Performance

It is important that you continually evaluate squad members' performances, contributions, and improvements. I will provide ideas on how to do that in regard to your cheerleaders' standards of conduct, skill improvement (along with your use of positive reinforcement), and games and competitions. Ongoing evaluations will help you build a program and build up your individual cheerleaders. Remember, you are coaching athletes.

Standards of Conduct

Cheerleaders are leaders who cheer. Each person on your squad is required to make a commitment to both leadership demands and skill development. Setting standards of conduct establishes your expectations.

Your cheerleading constitution embodies your standards of conduct. Each week, at each occurrence, you will need to address any issues that come up that depart from your constitution. Meet with individual squad members for personal discussions if you find that the standards of conduct are not met. Sometimes the standards of conduct are called a *cooperation contract*, and each cheerleader is asked to read and sign the document, agreeing to everything listed in it.

One way to help set the tone at the beginning of the year or season is to have your cheerleaders complete an Early Season Self-Evaluation (figure 12.1). A self-evaluation at the season's outset will help you get to know the foundation skill levels of your cheerleaders, learn their background experiences, preview their goals, assess their attitude about being on the squad, and find out areas of concern or confusion. I suggest that you select areas that reflect the focus of your program, adding additional areas that you feel are important. At the end of the season or year, meet with each cheerleader individu-

Early Season Self-Evaluation

Please fill out the following form as completely and honestly as possible. This information will help me as your cheerleading coach be able to serve you as an individual and our squad as a whole. This information will remain confidential.

Name: ______________________________

1. List prior experience in cheerleading, dance, or gymnastics: ______________________________
2. Describe any other related experience in sports or leadership positions: ______________________________
3. What are your personal skill goals for this season? ______________________________
4. What are your academic goals for this year? ______________________________
5. What do you do for personal conditioning? ______________________________
6. What are your strongest personal traits? ______________________________
7. What are your strongest cheering skills? ______________________________
8. What personality trait will you be trying to improve this year? ______________________________
9. What cheering skill area will you be trying to improve this year? ______________________________
10. How do you plan to make yourself a better cheerleader this year? ______________________________
11. How can you contribute to squad unity? ______________________________
12. Any questions about the standards of conduct listed in the cheerleader constitution? ______________________________

Figure 12.1 Early season self-evaluation.

ally to discuss what was written on the Early Season Self-Evaluation. This meeting provides a good opportunity for you to give feedback to each cheerleader about performance, contribution, and improvement.

PERSON TO PERSON

I like to meet with each cheerleader one-on-one. After I select the squad and begin to get everything organized, I read through all of the information provided on the Early Season Self-Evaluation. Then I have an informal meeting with each cheerleader so that each person has my undivided attention. My cheerleaders know they can talk to me about anything they want. During one of these meetings, a girl told me that she thought she had an eating disorder and didn't know what to do. Because of this meeting, I was able to discuss options with her and lead her to professional care.

Skill Improvement

Assessing skill improvement and then communicating your feedback will help build a successful program because you can help your cheerleaders gain confidence, learn proper practice and performance skills, and build pride through accomplishment.

There are many ways to communicate with your cheerleaders about their individual and squad skill improvement. The three most common are video viewing, verbal discussion, and written feedback. You will be able to assess improvement through these three avenues by comparison from preseason overall skill to postseason performance levels. You will also be able to assess improvement by observing the quality and quantity of specific cheering skills, as well as a rise in level of difficulty. I'll give you an overview of all three feedback methods so you can decide which ones you want to try.

Video Viewing

It has been said that a picture is worth a thousand words. When working with cheerleaders, sometimes one videotaping session can be worth hours of verbal coaching. Ask someone who knows how to videotape to attend a practice. Let your cheerleaders see the tape immediately after the filming so they can learn from their mistakes quickly. The most obvious areas to look for on the tape are body positions, levels, or angles, smoothness of transitions, facial expressions, voice quality, timing, and sharpness of motions. Continue the videotaping idea as many times as necessary until you can see marked improvement. Also, you may want to consider filming each person individually when working on jumps so that each person can see exactly what he or she needs to work on.

BEFORE AND AFTER

I decided that it would be interesting (and fun) to videotape my cheerleaders during the summer when they were just getting ready for the season, and then again after the football season. We focused on toe touch jumps, filming each person individually. There was one girl who was self-conscious about the low skill level of her toe touch jumps and who seemed nervous about the filming. After the initial filming session, she started spending more time working on her toe touch. After football season, when we filmed again, her jumps had improved dramatically. Her improved skill made a positive impact on her confidence level for the rest of the year.

Verbal Discussion

Verbal discussion about skill improvement embodies the role of coach. The more experienced you are as a coach, the better you will be able to use verbal communication to help your cheerleaders improve their skills. If you are new and need help in this area, use the sample Skill Improvement Form (figure 12.2) for verbal cues when discussing skill improvement with your cheerleaders. Use the form to take notes and then refer to it when discussing improvement areas. One thing you may want to remember during these sessions is to "keep it short and simple," or KISS. Don't try to improve everything at once. Select the most important areas and focus on a few. Also, let your cheerleaders take turns giving each other feedback on particular skill areas during practice. This is most effective when one person watches another and gives feedback privately.

Avoid criticizing individuals in front of the group, even when working on skill development. It's important not to embarrass anyone, hurt their feelings, or cause resentment or loss of confidence. You may have squad members who are shy, have low self-esteem, or are sensitive about their weaker

Skill Improvement Form

Evaluator: ______________________ Squad: ______________________

Date and location: ______________________

A ✓ next to the word means that more work is needed for improvement. A circle around a word means excellent or superior. Write comments or criticisms when needed. Please be as specific as possible.

Spirit

____ Smiles ____ Confidence ____ Eye contact ____ Leadership ____ Pep
____ Personality ____ Facial expression ____ Genuineness ____ Energy

Entrance or Taking the Floor

____ Spirit ____ Organization ____ Creativity ____ Crowd contact
____ Use of cheer area ____ Tumbling ____ Jumps ____ Excitement

Appearance

____ Hair back ____ No gum ____ No jewelry ____ Posture ____ Neatness
____ First impression ____ Clean uniforms ____ Minimal make-up

Chants/Leadership

____ Spirit ____ Organization ____ Communication ____ Effort to lead crowd
____ Creativity ____ Execution ____ Rhythm ____ Spacing ____ Personality

Voice

____ Low ____ Loud ____ Expression ____ Tone ____ Clarity ____ Control

Motions

____ Levels ____ Angles ____ Placement ____ Fists ____ Blades ____ Polish
____ Overextension ____ Control ____ Precision ____ Timing ____ Completion

Timing

____ Synchronization ____ Smoothness ____ Needs practice ____ Execution

Jumps

____ Height ____ Form ____ Toe pointed ____ Extension ____ Prep
____ Follow-through ____ Synchronization ____ Variety

(continued)

Figure 12.2 Skill improvement form.

Stunts/Mounts/Pyramids

____ Technique ____ Execution ____ Utilization ____ Eye contact

____ Safety techniques ____ Smoothness ____ Timing ____ Endings

Formations

____ Center ____ Spacing ____ Transitions ____ Variety

Exit

____ Spirit ____ Crowd response ____ Use of cheering area ____ Energy

____ Effectiveness ____ Strength ____ Organization

Overall Performance

____ Technique ____ Showmanship ____ Squad appeal ____ Degree of difficulty

____ Leadership ____ Crowd control ____ Personality projection

Figure 12.2 *(continued)*

skill areas. Arranging private meetings to discuss improvement areas will be less stressful for your cheerleaders. You will be able to help individual cheerleaders improve their skills by using positive reinforcement and by offering specific suggestions for improvement.

Written Feedback

One way to give written feedback to your cheerleaders is to print up a bunch of Skill Improvement Forms. Each cheerleading area can be printed on a separate form, or you may decide to print all areas on one large form. You can ask assistant coaches or private coaches to help evaluate your cheerleaders so that everyone receives quality feedback. Before the season actually starts, I would suggest giving written feedback once or twice a week. After the season starts, you may only provide written feedback following games. Take notes on the Skill Improvement Form, marking those areas that are strong and indicating weaker areas that need attention. You may want to alter the form so it better reflects your program.

Another idea I recommend is to fill out an End-of-Season Evaluation (figure 12.3). This evaluation form has both standards of conduct and skill improvement areas listed on it. This form can be discussed during individual meetings at the end of the year.

One way I have combined verbal and written evaluations is to divide my cheerleaders into two groups. The groups take turns cheering and being evaluated by the other group. They use the Skill Improvement Form to take notes, and then share what they wrote. I emphasize to them to share both good performance areas and areas that need improvement. This session works well because we only do it before the season begins, the session is not stressful, and everyone seems to have a good time. The cheerleaders truly want to help each other improve.

BLUE RIBBON ACHIEVEMENTS

I like my cheerleaders to evaluate each other during our early practices. I decided to make it more fun by having ribbons printed up that said Outstanding Improvement, Outstanding Spirit, Outstanding Cheering Skill, and Outstanding Leadership. I called them Achievement Ribbons and gave my cheerleaders some of each type of ribbon. After they evaluated each other in small groups, using the Skill Improvement Form, they presented a blue ribbon for each outstanding area. Not only did these Achievement Ribbons make the practices more fun, but my cheerleaders seemed to love having their own blue ribbons.

End-of-Season Evaluation

0...No attempt
1...Poor
2...Unacceptable
3...Could do better
4...Good
5...Excellent

____ **Arm motions:** Controlled, sharp, distinct movement

____ **Voice:** Loud and clear

____ **Jumps:** Uses jumps to show spirit, after cheers, and during games

____ **Respect for authority:** Accepts coach's requests without complaint

____ **Attendance:** Practices and games

____ **Dependability:** On time, ready mentally and physically

____ **Attitude:** Gets along with other cheerleaders, accepts new ideas

____ **Creativity:** Contributes new ideas to the squad

____ **Appearance:** Neat grooming, clean, follows appearance rules

____ **Spirit:** Supports the whole school, helps with extras

____ **Image:** Sets a good moral example

____ **Priorities:** Puts cheerleading before other nonacademic activities

____ **Improvement:** Makes honest effort to improve skills

____ **Commitment:** Does not waste practice time, gives 100 percent all the time

Figure 12.3 End-of-season evaluation.

Games and Competitions

Games and competitions also provide excellent opportunities for you to evaluate your cheerleaders' performance. When the adrenaline is pumping, you get to see the true level of performance possible from your cheerleaders. Cheering skills displayed during games and competitions are usually better than what you see at practice. I think this occurs because there is an audience and everyone wants to look good for the crowd. The cheerleaders try harder because of fear motivation (they don't want to make a mistake) and desire motivation (they want to be perfect and receive validation from others).

During a game, the responsibility of the cheerleading squad is to provide leadership in support of the school and the team. Even though skill is important during a game, the leadership and crowd involvement are of equal importance. When you are evaluating a performance during a game, make sure that you look at both skill and crowd involvement.

During a competition, the focus is on performance only, with little attention directed toward crowd involvement. After a cheerleading competition, it is important for you to go over the judging forms with your cheerleaders to discuss strong and weak areas. The judging forms reflect a numerical evaluation, and sometimes include written comments and criticisms. If possible, review a videotape of the actual competition performance so that you can validate the powerful areas and give encouragement for problem areas.

I know of cheerleading coaches who give their squads written evaluations after every game (one coach I know gives the squad an evaluation at halftime so they can improve during the second half). The Skill Improvement Form can be used as an evaluation form during games. Give your cheerleaders constant feedback on their effectiveness as crowd leaders and on their impact as skill-driven athletes. When evaluating crowd leadership, watch to see if fans are responding to cheers and chants and if there is a vocal display of unity. Notice if your squad is sensitive to the mood of the crowd and the action of the game. The squad's selection of cheers and chants should not only be responsive to the game action itself, but should also elicit crowd involvement.

Sometimes you can receive input from spectators at games. I recommend an idea I heard from a coach friend of mine: the Top Rate Card (figure 12.4), which can be printed on a five-by-eight unlined notecard. The coach would distribute some of these cards to spectators before each game; the identity of the evaluators was unknown to anyone but the coach. I have included a sample copy of the wording, but you can change the card to fit your needs.

How to Evaluate

First of all, balance the negative with the positive. Evaluation feedback should be simple and direct. When giving negative feedback or offering suggestions for improvement, make sure you criticize the performance and not the performer. Be specific about the skill area and what can be done to improve it. Do not focus on personal faults or make generalizations about character traits that contribute to performance. At the same time, be generous with praise for positive progress.

Top Rate Card

Dear Tiger Fan,

I am trying to encourage the cheerleaders to improve their crowd involvement and leadership skills. To this end, I have created an incentive award called the "Top Rate" cheerleader. The weekly winner will receive a special gift, and the cheerleader who receives the most votes throughout the season will receive a plaque. Will you please help me with this decision by voting for the cheerleader *at this event* whom you believe displays to the crowd the best enthusiasm, cheering skill, crowd leadership techniques, most jumps, best smiles, and overall best spirit? Please return this ballot to me at the end of this athletic contest or as soon as you have made your decision.

My decision for "Top Rate" cheerleader is ______________________________.

Positive and encouraging comments about your selection's performance and skill are welcome. Please place these on the reverse side. You may sign if you desire, but doing so is not mandatory for your vote to count. Thank you for your time and your encouragement to our cheerleaders to be their very best.

Coach signature ______________________________

Rater signature ______________________________

Figure 12.4 Top rate card.

Second, because most cheerleaders work very hard to do a good job and spend many hours supporting the school and the athletic program, never judge your squad as inferior to another squad in your school, city, county, or state. If you compare your squad to other squads, compare with strengths and not weaknesses. Each squad needs to feel unique. Each individual on a squad needs to feel that he or she contributes something special to the whole. When you are evaluating the standards of conduct, skill improvement, or performance at games and competitions, keep in mind that building confidence and positive attitudes is the most important part of your job.

Summary

Here are the key evaluation points outlined in this chapter:

- Use ongoing evaluations of your cheerleaders' performance to help build your program.
- Stay aware of how your individual cheerleaders are living up to the standards of conduct as outlined in your cheerleader constitution. Schedule personal meetings for feedback.
- Set the tone for the season or year by having your cheerleaders complete an Early Season Self-Evaluation.
- Communicate with your cheerleaders about skill improvement through video viewing, verbal discussion, and written feedback.
- Present written feedback to the squad or to individuals on the squad through coaching forms listing cheerleading skill areas.
- Meet with each cheerleader at the end of the year and discuss your evaluations as listed on an End-of-Season Evaluation.
- In your efforts to improve performance, take advantage of the judging forms, written comments, and videos that cheerleading competitions provide for your review.
- Give your cheerleaders continual feedback on their effectiveness at games as crowd leaders and their impact as skill-driven athletes.
- Ask spectators to rate cheerleaders during games, which allows you to receive feedback on the effectiveness of your cheerleaders' leadership.
- Use positive reinforcement to build confidence and positive attitudes.

Chapter 13

Evaluating Your Program

Conducting program evaluations will help you implement and fine-tune a successful program because you will learn best by trial-and-error . . . and by trial-and-success. If you don't stop to evaluate, you may continue to make the same mistakes, or you may not be fully aware of your program's strengths. Try to see your program as dynamic, changing, adjusting, and improving with each new experience.

Coaching cheerleaders is usually a year-round job, so you should be evaluating your program continuously. These evaluations may be formal (written) or informal (verbal feedback from your cheerleaders weekly). Even if you are constantly evaluating and upgrading your program on a weekly basis, you will still want to conduct a major end-of-season or end-of-year evaluation. In this chapter, I will provide ideas on how to conduct a thorough evaluation, along with hints on how to obtain feedback from your cheerleaders, their parents, your assistants, and the administration. I will also discuss evaluating your performance goals and effectiveness, the impact of your program on you personally, and a vision of commitment as you build for the future.

Postseason Evaluation

To thoroughly evaluate your program, you need feedback from your cheerleaders, their parents, your assistants, and the administration. The quality of their feedback and your dedication to improvement will have a direct impact on the success of your program.

Cheerleader Feedback

Your cheerleaders will usually be honest in their evaluations of your program, and will often give you excellent ideas on how to improve your effectiveness personally as a coach. One way to receive quality feedback at the end of the year is to schedule a personal meeting with each of your graduating seniors. Since they are leaving your program and will not be trying out again, they have nothing to fear by being frank. The meeting should be private and confidential. You can either make the meeting open-ended and unstructured, which may bring you more candid comments, or you can discuss the ideas and criticisms listed on the End-of-Year Questionnaire (figure 13.1). To get input from every cheerleader on your squad(s), give each person a version of this questionnaire, selecting the topics and questions that fit your program.

The feedback that you receive will give you a clear picture of how your program is perceived and how it can be improved. You will discover which parts of your program are well-received, what motivates your cheerleaders to work hard, and what changes your cheerleaders would like to see.

Courtesy of Mahomet-Seymour High School

In-Season Feedback

You don't have to wait until the end of the season or the end of the year to obtain quality feedback from your cheerleaders. I sometimes obtain feedback weekly by asking questions from two perspectives. First, I ask for feedback from the individual perspective:

- How do I feel about my attitude this week?
- How do I feel about my contribution this week?
- What could I have done better this week?
- How hard have I worked to improve my skills this week?
- Is there any aspect of the cheerleading program I am having problems with?

Next, I ask for feedback from a group perspective:

- How could we improve our effectiveness as leaders?
- What kind of squad unity did we have this week?
- How could we improve our squad's performance?
- Are we having any problems, challenges, or disappointments this week?

I like to obtain weekly feedback so I can stay on top of what's happening with individuals and within the group at the same time. This helps me to spot personality conflicts early, and attempt to establish a common ground of communication. Because of the wording of the questions, the cheerleaders come to realize that they are directly responsible for the quality of their experience. Squad members become actively involved not only in answering the difficult questions about building our program, but also in making positive things happen.

THE REAL WORLD

I have used weekly feedback sheets for many years because I like to give my cheerleaders the opportunity to share their thoughts and feelings with me on a regular basis. I call them my pink evaluation forms (pink evals for short) because I print them on pink paper. It was on these pink evals that I found out that two of the

End-of-Year Questionnaire

As you fill out the answers to the following areas, please be as honest and constructive as possible. Your input and feedback will help me improve the cheerleading program.

Rating system for items 1-10:

1	2	3	4	5	6	7
(Don't agree)						(Definitely agree)

____ 1. In terms of cheerleading skills, I learned many new things.

____ 2. My cheerleading skills improved a lot.

____ 3. I enjoyed cheering this season.

____ 4. My coach(es) helped me develop as a cheerleader.

____ 5. My coach(es) helped me develop as a person.

____ 6. I was treated fairly.

____ 7. I respected the rules of our constitution.

____ 8. Practices were well-organized, challenging, and fun.

____ 9. The cheerleaders are a respected organization in the school.

____ 10. I feel positive about how I contributed to the effectiveness of my squad.

Please write short answers for items 11-16.

11. The best thing about being a cheerleader in this program: ____________________

12. The worst thing about being a cheerleader in this program: ____________________

13. Explain changes you would make to improve or eliminate the worst things about the program (be specific): ____________________

14. What can the coach(es) do to make the program better than it was this past season?

____

15. Which goals did you achieve that you set for yourself this past season/year? ________

____

16. Which goals did you not achieve that you set for yourself this past season/year? _____

____

17. Rate the following areas according to their importance for you to become the best cheerleader you can be: (0-10 with 10 as high)

____ Goal setting ____ Handling adversity ____ Training or conditioning

____ Inner strength ____ Self-discipline ____ Technique ____ Leadership skills

Figure 13.1 End-of-year questionnaire.

members of my coed squad had started liking each other and wanted to date. Neither one of them wanted to cause a problem on the squad, so the three of us decided to have a meeting to discuss this issue. Since it had never come up in the past, we had no policy about intrasquad dating. As a result of the feedback I received on my pink evals, I was able to establish guidelines for dating on coed squads.

Parent Feedback

Open communication between yourself and your cheerleaders' parents is essential. I often have face-to-face meetings with the parents and sometimes send newsletters to keep them informed. Two reasons you need feedback from parents are that they usually provide most of the money that is spent on the cheerleader and they may also provide much of the transportation. Many parents want to keep up on all aspects of your program, and some may provide good ideas or insights for you.

If possible, obtain written feedback from the parents of your cheerleaders by asking for an evaluation of the following areas:

- Quality of communication and organization
- Strengths of the program
- Suggestions for improvement

RAILROAD

A coach friend of mine knew that things weren't going too well with her squads' parents, but she wasn't sure what to do next. The parents had been having their own private meetings with each other to which she had not been invited. Before she could find out the specific complaints or attempt to resolve the differences, a group of the parents printed up an inflammatory six-page letter full of complaints about her program (with some unwarranted personal criticism thrown in). The letter was mailed to each squad member's parents, the principal, the assistant principal, and the administrative officials for the district. So much damage was done because of the unfair nature of the complaints that my friend decided to resign. The train of negative thoughts had successfully pushed her off-track.

Pay close attention to what the parents have to say. They bring a unique perspective to the development of your program because they only evaluate everything secondhand (from the viewpoint of the cheerleader in their family) and they may not understand the complexity of your coaching job. Always make sure the parents know exactly what is expected of them and the cheerleader in their family. Weigh parent evaluations in the light of feedback from your cheerleaders. You will not be able to please everyone, and some parents are likely to bombard you with negatives. Don't let a few parents undermine your confidence as the coach. Remember that it's much easier to stand on the sidelines and criticize someone's program than to actually jump in and run the program. If you find that quite a few parents have listed an area of concern that you are surprised about, you may want to consider having a meeting with the parents or discussing the issue with an administrator at your school.

Assistant Coach Feedback

If you are lucky enough to have an assistant coach, you will want to spend some time discussing the effectiveness of the program. Your assistants are coaches-in-training and will greatly benefit from the feedback process themselves. They can bring insight and creativity into your program because their experience with the squad differs from your own.

Ask your assistants or managers to write answers to the following questions:

1. What were the program's positives from this season (or year)?
2. What were the program's negatives from this season (or year)?
3. How could the coach have done a better job?
4. What are your suggestions for program improvement?
5. What were your greatest strengths or contributions?
6. How could you have done a better job?

After the assistants have completed the questions, meet personally to discuss the answers. Listen and take notes: Some of your best ideas may come from these sessions. Not only are you receiving valuable input, you are also gaining an understanding of how to provide better leadership (by finding out strong and weak areas) and increased motivation (by praising and validating).

Administration Feedback

At the end of the season or the year, it is important that you meet with your principal or athletic director and the coaches of the teams that your cheerleaders support. You need feedback from the administrators and coaches who benefit from your cheerleaders' contributions to school spirit and crowd control. Adult leadership in your school should be in agreement about whether your program is consistent with the school's educational objectives.

Ask for feedback on the following areas:

- Organization and administration of the cheerleading program
- Effectiveness of the cheerleaders (leadership, crowd involvement, spirit)
- Attitude, conduct, and coaching philosophy

Your school's administrators need to understand the foundation of your program. Make sure they have copies of your constitution. If you are considering changes, discuss the changes with them to make sure you have their support. Share the results of your questionnaires with them. Open lines of communication will enable you to implement the program you want with the support of the administration. Establishing a cooperative relationship between you and your administrators will also help you if at any time an emergency or other serious matter should occur.

Self-Evaluation

This may be a difficult thing to do, but you need to evaluate your own effectiveness during the season or at the end of the year. The evaluation needs to be honest, specific, and thorough. You have probably already been asking yourself weekly "How could I do this better?" Now it's time to answer some very important questions. I recommend writing down, instead of just thinking about, the answers: The results will be much more powerful.

- How would I describe my attitude about my job as cheerleading coach?
- What do I like best about being the cheerleading coach?
- What do I like least about being the cheerleading coach?
- How effective was my communication with the cheerleaders, the parents, and the administrators this year?
- How effectively did I utilize my assistants?
- Which of my personal goals were met this year?
- Which of my personal goals were not met this year?
- What are my ideas for how to improve the program?
- What is an example of an incident that I feel good about?
- How could I improve my personal effectiveness as a leader?

I recommend a self-evaluation after each season that you coach. The answers will help you improve as a cheerleading coach . . . and grow as a person. They will prompt you to think about the impact of the program on you personally and force you to consider what went right or wrong, how you felt about your coaching role, how you could do a better job, and if you really want to remain a cheerleading coach. Self-inventory can be painful, but it is important to the success of your program.

Handling Program Demands

To be honest, the burnout rate of cheerleading coaches is quite high. The reasons center around the following areas: year-round responsibilities, little validation for the program, and low or nonexistent pay.

- Year-round responsibilities. Cheerleading coaches usually do not have a "season" because the cheerleaders serve the school year-round. They often have more than one squad to coordinate. Practices and games are outside of school hours, which means that the time demands are very high and the strain on family life is often unbearable.

- Little validation for the program. Traditionally, cheerleaders have been looked down on as "not really athletes," "not a team," "conceited girls in short skirts," or "effeminate males." These judgments do nothing but hurt cheerleading. Cheer programs seldom receive the kind of financial support that other athletic programs do in the school. They rarely have the use of good facilities and often have to raise all of their own money for uniforms, camp, supplies, and spirit items. Nor do cheerleading coaches commonly receive the appreciation they deserve from administrators or parents.

• Little or no pay. Cheerleading coaches usually receive some kind of salary for their job, but it's never what sport team coaches make, who, by the way, usually coach only one season. If the hours were computed and compared, the cheerleading coach, who serves athletes in the same way as sport team coaches, would receive an embarrassingly low pay by comparison. Many coaches are stung by the unfairness of this practice.

So why do cheerleading coaches serve? They do it because they care about the individuals who wish to cheer and they believe in the potential of the cheerleading program to make a positive impact on a young person's life. And they are willing to make personal sacrifices in order for young athletes to contribute to their schools and communities as cheerleaders.

What are some of the ways that tired, underpaid, overworked, dedicated cheerleading coaches can ease the strain? Here are some ideas that just might help:

- Organize a good parent support group. It can make your job easier.
- Set up a mandatory moratorium so that you have at least a six-week span in the summer where there are no cheerleading responsibilities.
- Delegate responsibilities to assistant coaches or squad managers.
- Enlist the assistance of a supportive administrator to help ease possible pressure from parents.
- Find a secretary in the office who will help you with your printing needs.
- Say no to added responsibilities for other school-related demands outside of the classroom.
- Collect positives! Read motivational stories, affirmations, and quotations.
- Focus on the benefits of building young lives.
- Be organized. You can definitely save time.
- Remember that giving is receiving. Your intangible rewards are great.
- Welcome change and greet each new challenge with a positive attitude.
- Write in a journal. This will help you relax, work off tension, or aid in your personal development.
- Take minivacations from all the demands of your coaching job.
- Start a Gratitude List and add to it daily if possible.
- Attend a motivational seminar to rejuvenate.
- Always be honest with your cheerleaders, their parents, and the administrators if you are struggling with some of the everyday pressures of handling the program.
- Give lots of hugs.

SEMINAR ON WHEELS

Working with cheerleaders can be physically and emotionally demanding. One of the things I do to keep myself calmed down and focused on what is truly important in my life is to listen to positive thinking tapes in my car. Zig Ziglar, Denis Waitley, and Wayne Dyer conduct personal seminars-on-wheels in my car quite often! The tapes inspire me not only to make positive choices in thought, word, and deed, but also to feel good about who I am and what I can contribute to the lives of young people. They help me to continue to say yes to being the best I can be.

Most people do not understand that serving as a cheerleading coach is tough as well as rewarding. Working with young athletes who are growing into special individuals provides an excitement that is difficult to describe. The reason that cheer coaches need to fill their hearts to capacity is because they will have more to give. Coaches touch the future.

Building for the Future

Cheerleaders serve their schools and communities as positive role models. They set standards and represent ideals for other students. Building for the future of your program is predicated on the close evaluation and analysis of these six key areas: squad traditions, reputation, contribution, effectiveness, procedure, and commitment.

Squad Traditions

Take a look at what traditions have continued from year to year, such as initiation (is

School Spirit Questionnaire

Please use the following rating system when responding to statements 1-10:

1 = Strongly disagree **2 = Disagree** **3 = Agree** **4 = Strongly agree**

_____ 1. The school spirit this year is better than last year.

_____ 2. The pep assemblies are better this year than last year.

_____ 3. Homecoming was better this year than last year.

_____ 4. Most students have a good attitude about our school.

_____ 5. The student council leaders are doing a good job of building spirit.

_____ 6. The cheerleaders are doing a good job of building spirit.

_____ 7. The faculty members are involved in building school spirit.

_____ 8. The administrators seem to support school spirit events.

_____ 9. School spirit can make a positive difference in our school.

_____ 10. Traditions at our school help build school spirit.

Please provide short answers to the following:

11. When was school spirit the best this year? ______________________________

____

____

12. How can the cheerleaders do a better job of building school spirit? __________

____

____

13. Does a Spirit Club help boost spirit? ______________________________

____

____

14. How can faculty or administrators help build spirit? ______________________

____

____

15. Do you have any other suggestions for building school spirit? ______________

____

____

____

Thanks for your time!

Figure 13.2 School spirit questionnaire.

it a special ceremony or similar to college hazing?). Does your squad have a special song, slogan, or symbol (make sure you approve of the selections)? Does your squad participate in a holiday gift exchange, community service project, or slumber party? Make sure you monitor the attitudes and activities of all the squad traditions that are perpetuated each year. They need to fall within your guidelines and philosophy, to be positive, and to promote the program.

Reputation

Find out how the cheerleaders are perceived in the school. Make a point to talk with teachers and administrators about the historical reputation of the cheerleading program in your school, and listen for information about individuals who may bring your program down because of a "bad reputation." You can assess this area with teacher evaluation forms and informal talks with students and parents.

Contribution

Many cheerleading squads are involved in community service projects, such as hosting a community cheer clinic for elementary children. This particular event not only provides positive fun for the kids, but also is a wonderful opportunity for your cheerleaders to take on new responsibilities and gain additional leadership experience. I recommend that your cheerleaders select at least one service project (chapter 4 lists some suggestions) to build good public relations and program enhancement at the same time.

Effectiveness

How does the squad fulfill its leadership mission in the school? One way to obtain immediate feedback is to administer a School Spirit Questionnaire so that students can evaluate the effectiveness of your squad. An example is provided in figure 13.2. You can also get feedback from parent groups, band boosters, community organizations, and parents who attend the games. I have seen highly skilled cheerleading squads who performed but did not lead. Your squad needs both skill and leadership to be effective, and you need to obtain feedback consistently to improve your program.

Procedure

How well is your program organized and administered? Information from your cheerleaders, assistants, parents, and administrators will help you evaluate your effectiveness. Be flexible, keep a good attitude, and proceed with confidence.

Commitment

Am I truly committed to building people through cheerleading? The results of your self-evaluation will help you answer this question. Stay alert to your true feelings, possible burnout, and general attitude. Do you plan special events "above and beyond the call of duty," or are you just "putting in time?" Commitment can be measured on the outside by going the extra mile, and on the inside by the amount of love in your heart.

You build the future of your program as you build yourself as a person. Your program is an extension of the inner you and an expression of your commitment to educational values. Since extracurricular activity is the other half of education, a good coach balances academic and athletic expression and accomplishment within the context of the educational mission.

Summary

These are the key points to consider when you are evaluating your program:

- Coaching cheerleaders is usually a year-round job, so you should be evaluating your program continuously.
- One way to receive feedback about your program from your cheerleaders is to ask them to fill out an End-of-Year Questionnaire.

- Try to get feedback from the parents of your cheerleaders about the strengths of your program and any suggestions for improvement.
- If you have assistant coaches, ask them for feedback about how the program could be improved.
- Personal meetings with cheerleaders, coaches, and administrators is one way to receive quality information about the effectiveness of your program.
- At the end of the season or year, you need to conduct your own serious and honest self-evaluation.
- The main reasons for cheerleader coach burnout are the stress of year-round responsibilities, little validation for the program, and little or no pay.
- There are many ways that tired, underpaid, overworked, dedicated cheerleading coaches can ease the strain of their job, such as having a good parent support group, delegating responsibilities to assistant coaches or squad managers, reading motivational literature, taking minivacations, or writing in a personal journal.
- When building for the future of your program, evaluate the following areas: squad traditions, reputation, contribution, effectiveness, procedure, and commitment.

Appendix A

Writing Your Cheerleading Constitution

To establish and maintain a strong cheerleading program, you will need to put everything in writing. Writing things down gives everyone the opportunity to read, understand, discuss, and question all aspects of your program. You can call your document your Constitution, Rules and Regulations, Expectations for Cheerleaders, Guidelines for the Cheerleading Program, team handbook, team policies, or something similar. After your have drafted your document, have it approved by your administration before you distribute it to parents and candidates.

The structure and content of your cheerleader constitution will depend on many things: the size of your school, enrollment, school traditions, student support, available talent, athletic programs, religious beliefs, and administration policies. The following is a list of possible components that you should consider as you begin to construct your constitution. Select your topics and develop them to reflect the focus of your program.

Purpose of Cheerleading

1. The cheerleaders shall promote and uphold school spirit.
2. They shall encourage good sportsmanship among students and adults.
3. They shall promote unification of the crowd's involvement during athletic events.
4. They shall strive to build better relationships between schools.
5. They shall strive to uphold the highest personal, as well as cheerleading, standards.

Values of Cheerleading

1. Leadership
2. Physical fitness, coordination, healthy lifestyle
3. Respect, courtesy, tolerance, self-control
4. Sportsmanship and citizenship
5. Sports appreciation

6. Responsibility, patience, respect
7. Communication skills
8. Self-confidence and personal expression
9. Character
10. Moral development

Squad Membership

1. List male and female varsity and junior varsity sports.
2. Decide how many sports each squad will cheer for.
3. Decide how many will be on each cheerleading squad to successfully support all teams.
4. Decide what classes will be represented on each squad.
5. If responsibilities are shared, list who cheers when.

General Cheerleader Guidelines

1. Must attend practice and show cooperation with other cheerleaders and the coach.
2. Must know the cheers, chants, and routines for all games and performances.
3. Must adhere to the rules as listed in the constitution.
4. Should keep a good attitude about improving cheerleading skills.
5. Should take the responsibility of providing positive leadership both when cheering and when not cheering.
6. Should always show respect and be courteous to faculty members, administration, officials, coaches, players, and visitors.
7. Should be aware of their appearance at all times, using good grooming and dress habits.
8. Must follow the safety rules as listed in the National Federation's *High School Spirit Rules Book*.
9. Should strive to be modest in victory and gracious in defeat.
10. Should always remember that their primary responsibility is to support the athletic program.

Tryouts

Time and Place

List exactly when tryouts will be held for each squad.

Eligibility

1. Must return all forms:
   - Parental notification and permission form
   - Health form
   - Insurance form
   - Sign-up form
   - Grades
   - Other forms
2. Must maintain certain grade average individually.
3. Must attend pre-tryout training sessions.
4. Should have good ratings on teacher assessments.
5. Should have a good Pep or Spirit Club standing.

Skills and Procedures

List exactly what is involved during the tryout sessions:

1. Group cheer (predetermined)
2. Individual cheer (predetermined)
3. Original cheer
4. Chants (group or individual, predetermined or original)
5. Jumps (list specific)
6. Extra skills, such as splits, tumbling, etc.
7. Questions and answers
8. Interview
9. Spirit posters and ideas

Judges

If you are not selecting your squad independently, decide which groups or individuals will serve as judges:

1. Teachers and coaches
2. Pep or Spirit Club members or officers
3. Outgoing senior cheerleaders
4. Cheerleading coaches from your area
5. Outside judges, such as professional instructors from cheerleading companies
6. College cheerleaders
7. Student Council representatives
8. Other student body representatives

Judging and Point System

List the areas that will be judged and how many points for each area (a five-point scale is very effective):

1. Five points: excellent, outstanding, perfect

2. Four points: very good, but not perfect, superior
3. Three points: average-to-good, needs improvement
4. Two points: fair, needs a lot of work
5. One point: poor, inadequate

Captain or Head Cheerleader

1. Provide information about whether you will have a captain or head cheerleader (or more than one), or rotate responsibilities.
2. If having a captain or head cheerleader, decide and list how that person will be selected:
    - Appointed by the coach
    - Voted on by the squad
    - Based on seniority
    - Combination of the above
3. List basic responsibilities:
    - Call practices.
    - Start cheers and chants at games.
    - Work closely with coach.
    - Be responsible for equipment.
    - Provide communication and organization for entire squad.
    - Fulfill any other designated duties.

Coach Responsibilities

1. Attend and carefully supervise all practices and performances.
2. Keep injury records.
3. Have an emergency plan (and phone numbers) in case of accident or injury.
4. Complete sport first aid and CPR training.
5. Keep skill charts as a record of progressions followed.
6. Help write the cheerleader constitution.
7. Work with the administration.
8. Communicate with the parents.
9. Prepare and conduct tryouts.
10. Counsel squad members when needed.
11. Keep a notebook with information about every aspect of your program.
12. Have first aid kit at all practices and games.
13. Attend camps, clinics, workshops, and seminars to improve skills.
14. Keep up-to-date with books and videos to improve program.
15. Provide motivation, consistency, and organization for the squad.
16. Decide how you will handle the following circumstances, which may be evaluated by you alone or with input from the principal or a student panel:
    - Undesirable or immoral behavior
    - Sloppy appearance or habits
    - Undesirable language or gestures
    - Failure to uphold constitution
    - Violations of rules and regulations
    - Anything that harms the reputation of the program or the school
17. Perform other responsibilities as decided upon.

Cheerleader Conduct and Responsibilities

1. A cheerleader shall cooperate with the captain, the coach, the game officials, and other squad members.
2. A cheerleader should be enthusiastic, prepared, and in command of the situation at all times.
3. A cheerleader should not eat, drink, or chew gum while on the field or court.
4. A cheerleader should not sit in the stands or leave the squad until the end of the game.
5. A cheerleader should promote good sportsmanship and school spirit through cooperation with other students, faculty, and administrators.
6. Cheerleaders should plan pep rallies, contribute spirit ideas, and help control the attitudes of the crowd.
7. A grade point average of ___________ should be maintained (usually 2.0 for athletes).

Uniforms and Appearance

1. List what the school pays for.
2. List what each individual pays for.
3. Make each person responsible for the care of the uniform.
4. Describe length and style guidelines (and who decides on the uniform).
5. Wear uniforms only in conjunction with school events.
6. Keep hair out of the face at all times.
7. Prohibit wearing jewelry to practices or games.

8. Make-up should be minimal, subject to approval by coach.
9. List care and equipment of uniforms.
10. List any other special provisions regarding uniforms and appearance.

Games

List all games and arrival times, and which squad cheers for each game.

Practice Sessions

1. Require attendance at all practices.
2. List policy for missing a practice or being late.
3. List days and times of summer and school-year practices.
4. List basic organization for practices.
5. List ongoing conditioning, weight training, and strengthening programs that are part of your program.

Transportation

List school policy and whether a permission slip needs to be signed. The school should provide transportation. If for some reason your school does not provide transportation for your cheerleaders, ask the parents to talk to the athletic director. Transportation for the cheerleaders is a liability issue that the school needs to address. As the coach, you have the responsibility of arranging for transportation to away games and it should be in a school vehicle (even if you are the one driving).

Point System: Merits

1. List how points can be earned during the year.
2. List what award or letter will be presented after so many points.

Point System: Demerits

1. List how many points will be charged to a cheerleader for infringement of the rules as listed.
2. List how many points it takes to be benched or removed from the squad.
3. List grievance procedure.

Special Events

List pep rallies, parades, exhibitions, or community service projects the squad will be involved with.

Competition

Describe your position on cheerleading competition. If your squad will compete, share your philosophy of competition and detail how you will prepare, what competitions you will enter, and whether it is a mandatory part of your program.

Fundraising Responsibilities

Make it clear whether your cheerleaders will be involved in fundraising activities during the summer and throughout the year and list all scheduled or traditional events.

Safety Rules

List the safety rules that have been adopted by your state, your district, your conference, and your league. Many state high school associations have adopted the safety rules of the National Federation of State High School Associations. It is important that your cheerleaders know that you expect them to abide by these safety rules at all times.

Cheerleader Duties

If you have decided to rotate cheerleaders to different responsibilities during the year, list the requirements for positions in areas such as conditioning, publicity, corresponding secretary, squad coordinator, treasurer, special events, spirit coordinator, historian, creative coordinator, point keeper.

Camps and Clinics

Discuss whether your squad will be attending camps and clinics and, if so, the dates and financial obligations.

Awards and Banquet

Decide whether your cheerleaders will be part of an athletic awards banquet and what they must do to letter.

Personal Areas

Decide how you will handle the following issues:

1. Attitude and the ability to get along with coach and squad members
2. Conflicts with other activities
3. Conflicts with work outside of school
4. Resignation
5. Injury or illness leaves
6. Pregnancy
7. Financial hardship

Appendix B

Cheerleading Resources

Private Cheerleading Companies

The following is an incomplete list of national and regional cheerleading companies. Many local companies will mail information to cheer coaches, so look for brochures from local companies, as well.

Championship Cheerleading
2408 Links Way
Vista, CA 92083

Cheer Limited
5851 Ramsey St.
Fayetteville, NC 28311

Eastern Cheerleaders Association
P.O. Box 475
South Hill, VA 23970

Elite Cheerleading Organization
816 Grandview Ave.
Pittsburgh, PA 15211

National Cheerleaders Association
P.O. Box 660359
Dallas, TX 75266-0359

Nationwide Cheerleaders
1831 Route 286 South
Indiana, PA 15701

U.S. Spiritleaders
3591 Cerritos Ave.
Los Alamitos, CA 90720

Unity Spirit Action
5900 Kirkwood Cir.
Minneapolis, MN 55442

Universal Cheerleaders Association
2525 Horizon Lake Dr., Ste. 1
Memphis, TN 38133

United Spirit Association
521 E. Weddell Dr., Ste. 110
Sunnyvale, CA 94089-2114

United Performing Association
2720 Nevada Ave. North
Minneapolis, MN 55427

World Cheerleading Association
14006 W. 107th St.
Lenexa, KS 66215

Publications

American Cheerleader Magazine
Lifestyle Publications, Inc.
350 W. 50th St., Ste. 2AA
New York, NY 10019

Let's Cheer Magazine
Kay Crawford
1212 Ynez
Redondo Beach, CA 90277

Uniform Companies

The following are national companies which provide uniforms and other cheerleading supplies. Many regional and local companies also exist, so look for mailings from local and regional companies in your area.

Cheer In Style
P.O. Box 207
Lee's Summit, MO 64063

Cheerleader/Danz Team
5155 Vine St., #617
Lincoln, NE 68504

Cranbarry Cheerleading, Inc.
130 Condor St., Box 488
Boston, MA 02128

Elite
P.O. Box 2077
LaCrosse, WI 54602

Hibbard's Pep Supply
4983 Santa Anita Ave.
Temple City, CA 91780

Varsity Spirit Fashions
2525 Horizon Lake Dr., Ste. 1
Memphis, TN 38133

Index

U

V

W

Y

Z

About the Author

Linda Rae Chappell has been coaching amateur and professional cheerleaders for more than 25 years.

After cheering for her high school and college, Linda started her own business at the age of 23, the Dynamic Cheerleaders Association, Inc. (DCA). With DCA she established cheerleading camps at college and university campuses in 30 states, trained her staff of some 350 college cheerleaders to conduct the camps, and conducted six national cheerleading championships. Through DCA she also established a national mail-order business for cheerleaders' clothing, accessories, and educational materials.

Linda has presented numerous seminars, clinics, and workshops for cheerleading coaches and advisors, and has delivered motivational seminars at national coaches conventions.

A prolific author, she has written on spirit raising and leadership, sportsmanship, fundraising, and coach training. Her first book, *The Spirit Book*, has been referred to by many coaches as the "cheerleading Bible." She also has supervised production of books and videos on safety rules for the National Federation of State High School Associations, and she has produced and directed instructional videos in cheer and dance.

In 1986 Linda established a coed cheerleading squad for the Kansas City Chiefs (NFL football team), coaching the squad until 1990.

Linda, a member of the Missouri Cheerleading Coaches Association, is a former cheerleading director for the Midwest Missouri Youth Sports Association. In 1987 she earned her master's in educational administration from the University of Missouri.

Related Books For Cheerleaders

Second Edition

SPORT STRETCH

311 Stretches for 41 Sports

MICHAEL J. ALTER

1998 • 232 pp • Paperback
ISBN 0-88011-823-7 • $16.95 ($24.95 Canadian)

Take the guesswork out of stretching for your sport. The most effective exercises are presented, with the 12 best highlighted—perfect for warming up and cooling down. Or, work on your overall flexibility with the special "All Star" stretches—the single most effective stretches for 28 different muscle groups.

Nancy Clark's

SPORTS NUTRITION GUIDEBOOK

Second Edition

Eating to Fuel Your Active Lifestyle

Over 150,000 Sold!

NANCY CLARK, MS, RD

1997 • 464 pp • Paperback
ISBN 0-87322-730-1 • $16.95 ($24.95 Canadian)

This revised and expanded edition provides how-to food suggestions that make it easy to create a winning diet for high energy, peak performance, and lifelong health. The book also provides 131 nutritious recipes.

FUNDRAISING FOR SPORT AND RECREATION

STEP-BY-STEP PLANS FOR 70 SUCCESSFUL EVENTS

WILLIAM F. STIER, JR.

1994 • 216 pp • Paperback
ISBN 0-87322-400-0 • $17.00 ($25.50 Canadian)

This cookbook-style guide is filled with complete, step-by-step instructions for 70 fundraising events. For every event the book lists the net profit possibilities, complexity, people needed, and seed money required.

Prices are subject to change.

HUMAN KINETICS
The Premier Publisher for Sports & Fitness
www.humankinetics.com

To request more information or to place your order, U.S. customers **call TOLL FREE 1-800-747-4457.** Customers outside the U.S. use the appropriate telephone number/address shown in the front of this book.

2335

12/99